Table of Contents

Understanding Maps 2
   Locating the Continents and Oceans 3
   Locating the Continents and Oceans
      (Continued) 4
   Map Projections 5
   Map Projections (Continued) 6
   Temperature Zones 7
   World Time Zones 8
   World Time Zones (Continued) 9
   Using Scale 10

The Stone Age 11
   Sites of Human Remains 12
   Paleolithic Age 13
   Primitive People and Their Art 14

Ancient Egypt and Mesopotamia 15
   Permanent Cities 16
   Fertile Crescent 17
   Ancient Egypt 18

Early Civilizations in the Near East 19
   Twelve Tribes of Israel 20
   Twelve Tribes of Israel (Continued) 21
   Growth of the Persian Empire 22
   Phoenician Settlements 23

Ancient Greece 24
   Greek City-States 25
   Settlements of Ancient Greece 26
   The Athenian Empire 27
   Alexander's Conquests: 336-323 B.C. 28
   Alexander's Conquests: 336-323 B.C.
      (Continued) 29
   Alexander the Great's Empire 30

Roman Empire 31
   Roman Highways 32
   Empire of Augustus (27 B.C.-A.D. 14) 33
   The Roman Empire A.D. 117 34

Europe in the Middle Ages 35
   Barbarian Invaders 36
   Europe in A.D. 400 37
   Germanic States A.D. 526 38
   England A.D. 800 39
   Charlemagne's Empire A.D. 800 40

*The Birthplace and Spread
   of Three Religions* 41
   Ancient Israel 42
   Ancient Israel (Continued) 43
   Palestine in the First Century A.D. 44
   Spread of Christianity 45
   Spread of Christianity (Continued) 46
   Expansion of Islam to A.D. 750 47

China and India 48
   The Han Empire, First Century B.C. 49
   Empire of the Mongols 50
   Empire of the Mongols (Continued) 51
   Empires in India 52

The African Continent 53
   Explorers in Africa 54
   Sub-Saharan Africa 55
   Cultural Areas of Africa 56
   Cultural Areas of Africa (Continued) 57

Trade Routes 58
   Egyptian Trade Routes 59
   The Economy of the Hellenistic Period 60
   Economic Life in the Roman Empire 61
   Economic Life in the Roman Empire
      (Continued) 62
   African Trade Routes 63

Western Hemisphere 64
   Early People in the Americas 65
   Native Cultures of America 66

The World Today 67
   North America 68
   South America 69
   Australia (and New Zealand) 70
   Africa 71
   Europe 72
   Asia 73
Glossary 74-75
Answer Key 76-80

Understanding Maps

Concept: Maps are necessary tools in today's world.

Objective: To help students understand the different types of information maps supply.

Vocabulary: map, continent, hemisphere, map projection, mercator projection, equal-area map, latitude, longitude, equator, prime meridian, temperate, torrid, frigid, time zone, scale

Background Information:
- The surface of the earth is divided into land and water. The earth is about 70% water (oceans) and 30% land (continents).
- The earth is often subdivided into four hemispheres – Eastern, Western, Northern, and Southern.
- Using meridians and parallels, cartographers have different ways to show the round earth on a flat piece of paper. These methods are called map projections. A map should be drawn on a projection that most accurately shows the required features on that particular map. Every flat map has some distortion.
- Temperature zones are determined by the closeness of the Earth's surface to the sun.
- The earth rotates on its axis once every 24 hours. All 360° of the earth's circumference pass beneath the sun in that time. In one hour, 15° of the earth pass beneath the sun (1/24 x 360° = 15°). Most maps show longitude lines every 15°.
- Using a scale is the cartographer's way to reduce the earth's surface proportionately on a piece of paper. Scales use one unit of measurement to stand for another unit of measurement.

Teaching Suggestions

1. This chapter is a review of facts and topics that students at this level should already be familiar with. Use a globe and/or large maps of the world to remind the class about hemispheres before using the activity pages *Locating the Continents and Oceans*.

2. Tell the students that different map projections are used to portray different types of information. If possible, show students large Mercator and equal-area maps. The purpose of a Mercator projection is to accurately determine directions. Equal-area maps show the size of land and water areas accurately. The activity page *Map Projections* may be used at this point.

3. Show the class a large map which shows the equator, Tropics of Cancer and Capricorn, and the Arctic and Antarctic circles. Talk to them about how differences in latitude affect climate. Explain that the amount of heat a city or country receives depends on its distance from the equator and its altitude. Students will need crayons or markers to complete *Temperature Zones*.

4. Before beginning *World Time Zones*, explain to the class that each degree of longitude equals 4 minutes; therefore, 15 degrees equal one hour. For this activity, the prime meridian (0°) is 12 noon. This concept is difficult for many students. You may need to give students some help on an individual basis. Go over the note on the map page explaining how time changes as one moves east or west.

5. Tell the students they must measure from dot-to-dot on the activity page *Using Scale*. Each distance should be rounded to the nearest 50 miles. Students may use a ruler or a piece of paper to measure the distance between cities.

Additional Activities

1. Have students complete a chart which shows the correct temperature zone for each of the countries in North and South America. If a country falls within more than one zone, list the country in both zones.

2. Drawing a Mercator map of the classroom will help the students understand the difference between a Mercator projection and other projections. A Mercator projection should show a student's desk and a teacher's desk to be about the same size. An equal-area map would show the difference in size.

3. For additional practice with time zones, make copies of a time zone map of the United States. Ask the same types of questions as found on the *World Time Zones* activity page.

Locating the Continents and Oceans

Name _____

Use these maps to complete this page and page 4. Note: Some continents are located in more than one hemisphere.

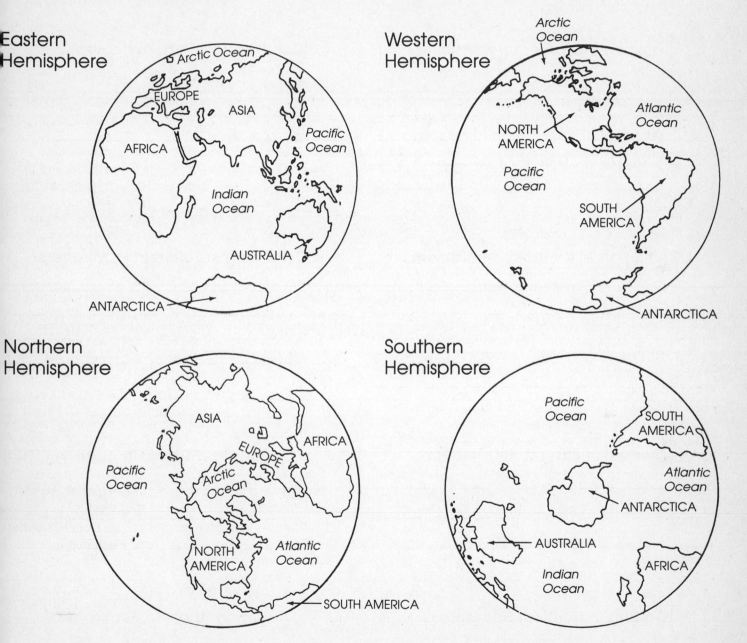

1. Which continent is found in both the Eastern and Western hemispheres?

_____

2. Which hemisphere does not include Antarctica? _____

3. Color the continent located entirely in the Western and Northern hemispheres red.

4. Color the continent located entirely in the Eastern and Southern hemispheres blue.

Locating the Continents and Oceans

(Continued)   Name _____

Use with page 3. Fill in the blanks.

Continents in Eastern Hemisphere

_____
_____
_____
_____
_____

Continents in Western Hemisphere

_____
_____
_____
_____

Continents in Northern Hemisphere

_____
_____
_____
_____
_____

Continents in Southern Hemisphere

_____
_____
_____
_____

Oceans in Eastern Hemisphere

_____
_____
_____

Oceans in Western Hemisphere

_____
_____
_____

Oceans in Northern Hemisphere

_____
_____
_____

Oceans in Southern Hemisphere

_____
_____
_____

Map Projections

Name _____

Use with page 6.

MERCATOR

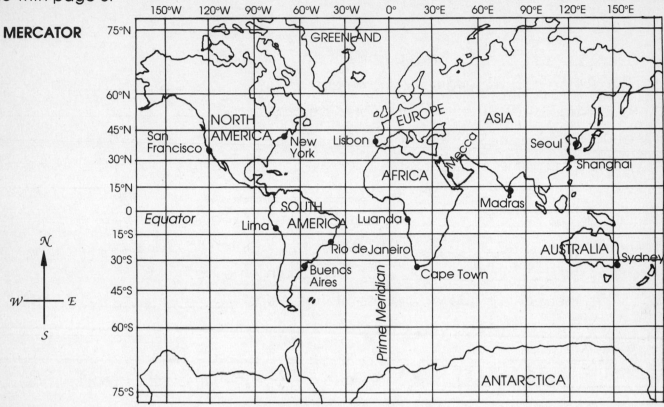

A Mercator map is best for finding directions.

EQUAL-AREA

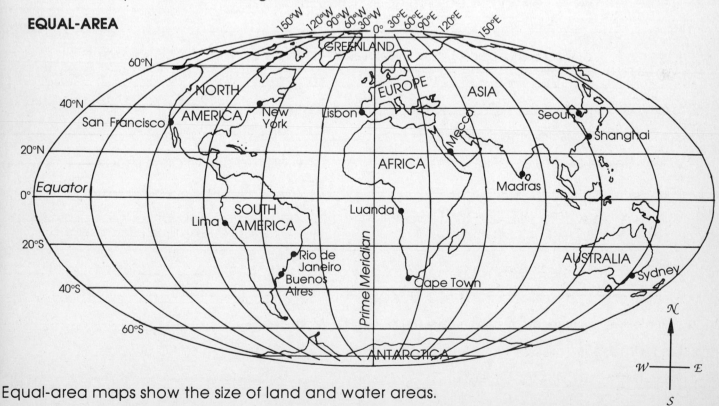

Equal-area maps show the size of land and water areas.

Map Projections (Continued)

Name _____

Use the two maps on page 5 to answer the questions below.

1. A _____ map is best for finding directions.

2. The size of land and water areas is shown best on an _____ map.

3. On which map does Greenland appear to be very large? _____

4. The equator is _____ latitude.

5. The prime meridian is _____ longitude.

6. Seoul is which direction from Shanghai? _____

7. The city of _____ is in southeastern Australia.

8. The city of _____ is located on the southern tip of Africa.

9. Lima is on the _____ coast of South America.

10. Name the lines of longitude which pass through Africa. _____

11. Name the three continents the prime meridian passes through. _____

_____

12. The _____ latitude line runs through Antarctica on the Mercator projection map.

13. Lisbon is located between which two lines of longitude? _____

14. Name the two cities on the eastern coast of South America. _____

_____

15. Mecca is located between which two lines of latitude on the Mercator map?

_____

16. Luanda is on the _____ coast of Africa.

17. San Francisco is located closest to the _____ line of longitude.

18. Which lines of latitude pass through South America on the equal-area map?

_____

19. Which map would you use to decide if Africa or South America is larger? _____

_____

20. Which map projection shows the "true" size of Antarctica? _____

21. On which map projection does Africa seem larger? _____

22. Which map projection shows the "true" size of Australia? _____

23. Label these bodies of water on both maps: Pacific Ocean, Atlantic Ocean,

    Indian Ocean, Arctic Ocean

Temperature Zones

Name _____

Use this map and map key to answer the questions.

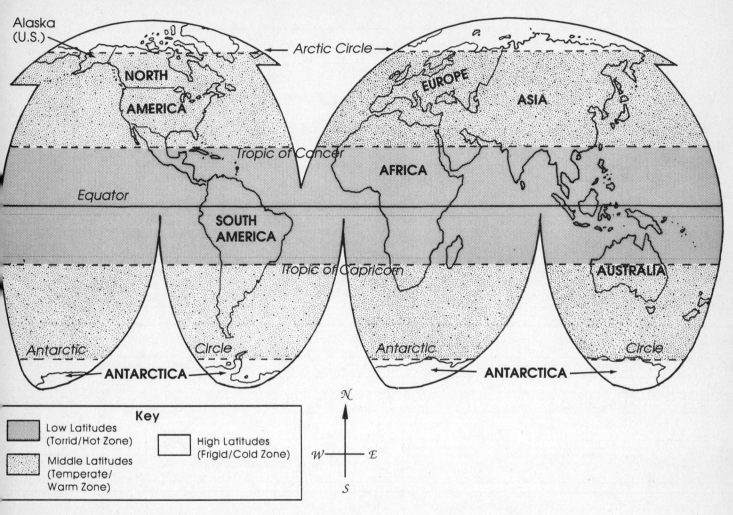

Key

Low Latitudes (Torrid/Hot Zone)

Middle Latitudes (Temperate/ Warm Zone)

High Latitudes (Frigid/Cold Zone)

1. The temperate zone is also known as the _____ zone.

2. Most of North America is found in the _____ latitudes.

3. Australia is divided between which two latitudes? _____

4. The Tropic of Capricorn passes through which three continents? _____

_____

5. The _____ Circle passes through northern Asia.

6. The Tropic of Cancer passes through which three continents? _____

_____

7. Most of Europe is located in the _____ latitudes.

8. Name the continent located almost entirely in the frigid zone. _____

9. What type of climate would you expect to find in northern South America? _____

10. Use crayons or markers to color each of the temperature zones a different color.

World Time Zones

Name _____

Use with page 9.

Note: Time zones start at the Prime Meridian and divide the world into 24 parts. When going west, time is set back one hour for each time zone crossed. When going east, time goes forward one hour for each time zone crossed.

Time Map of the World

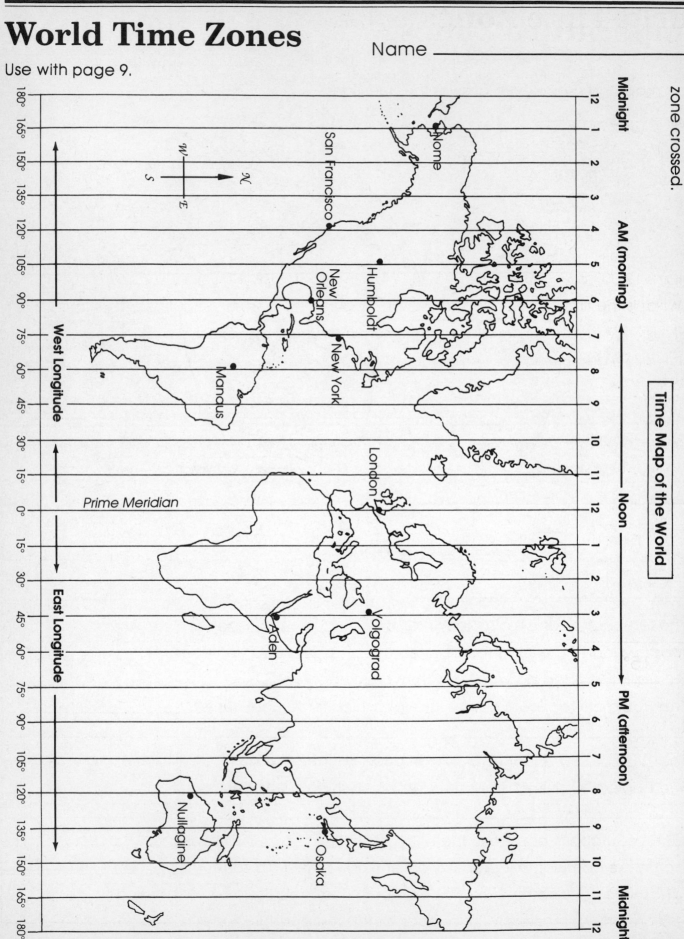

World Time Zones (Continued)

Name _____

Use the map on page 8 to answer the questions and complete the table.

1. On the map each line of longitude equals _____ hour.

2. What time does the prime meridian represent? _____

3. Which line of longitude shows 12:00 midnight? _____

4. Are the east longitude lines left of the prime meridian? _____

5. Which direction do the longitude lines on the right of the prime meridian represent?

_____

6. If it is 12:00 noon in London, what time is it in San Francisco? _____

7. What is the time difference between Nullagine and Osaka? _____

8. If it is 3 PM in Aden, what time is it in New Orleans? _____

9. If it is 3 PM in Volgograd, what time is it in Nome? _____

10. If it is 5 AM in Humboldt, what time is it in Osaka? _____

11. How many hours difference is there between San Francisco and Volgograd? _____

12. How many hours difference is there between Manaus and Nullagine? _____

13. Using the information on the map, complete this chart.

Longitude	Time	Longitude	Time
0°	12:00 noon	135°E	
90°W	6 AM	165°W	
	8 PM	60°E	4 PM
15°E		180°	12:00 midnight
135°W		75°E	5 PM
30°W	10 AM		10 PM
105°E	7 PM	105°W	
45°E		15°W	11 AM
75°W	7 AM		4 AM
	2 AM	30°E	2 PM

Using Scale

Name _____

Using this map and the scale of miles, complete the table of approximate distances between cities.

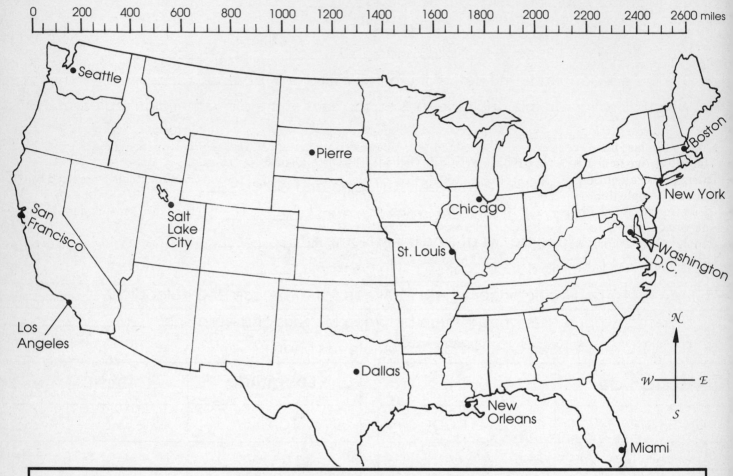

Distance in Miles Between Cities				
Cities	Boston	Miami	St. Louis	Chicago
Dallas				
New Orleans				
Los Angeles				
Seattle				
New York				
Washington				
Pierre				
Salt Lake City				
San Francisco				

The Stone Age

Concept: The early period of history when people made tools and weapons mainly from stone is known as the Stone Age.

Objective: To help students to understand that the Stone Age is the early stage of cultural development when most tools and weapons were made of stone.

Vocabulary: Stone Age, Homo sapiens, Homo erectus, Australopithecus, flake tool, ice sheet, hominid, animal husbandry

Background Information:
- The Stone Age got its name because people survived during this period mainly by hunting with stone tools. During the last phase of the Stone Age (Neolithic), however, an agricultural way of life was introduced.
- The Stone Age is divided into three periods—Paleolithic, Mesolithic, and Neolithic.
- During the Paleolithic period, ice sheets advanced and receded over much of the earth. Stone tools were used by hunters. People discovered how to use fire.
- Climatic conditions improved during the Mesolithic period. The glacial ice receded. Many different kinds of tools and weapons made of stone, bones, and antlers came into use.
- People began to farm and domesticate animals during the Neolithic period. The use of the wheel, plow, and draft animals spread. Carpentry, pottery making, and textile weaving developed.

Teaching Suggestions

1. Before handing out any activity pages, have the students define the vocabulary words. Most of the words will be new to them. The activity page *Sites of Human Remains* shows the location of archaeological sites in Africa, Europe, and Asia. Students will need to refer to a modern-day map of the world.

2. Use a large map or globe to show the extent of area covered by glaciers. *Paleolithic Age* shows the locations where flake tools and handaxes were made and used.

3. *Primitive People and Their Art* asks the students to use a map and a time line. Tell the students that a time line is just another way to present information. Provide the students with a map of the world for reference.

Additional Activities

1. Have the students create a time line for their own lives. The students' time lines should all be different since they will choose events unique to their own families. Examples: year of birth, date began to walk/talk, learned to swim, started school, family vacations, camps, moved to a new house or town, etc.

2. Have the class create a time line for your state. This could be done on a long sheet of paper and placed on a wall. Assign every 5 years to two students. Some information may not seem overly important, but the object of the activity is for students to research and make time lines.

3. Divide the class into groups of three or four students. Each group will brainstorm a list of 15 modern tools it would not like to live without. Have each group reduce its list to 10 tools and then to five tools. Compare the final lists by placing them on a wall chart.

Sites of Human Remains

Name _____

This map shows the location of sites where some primitive human remains were located. These remains are from the period of history known as the Stone Age. Use this map, the map key, and a modern-day map of the world to answer the questions below.

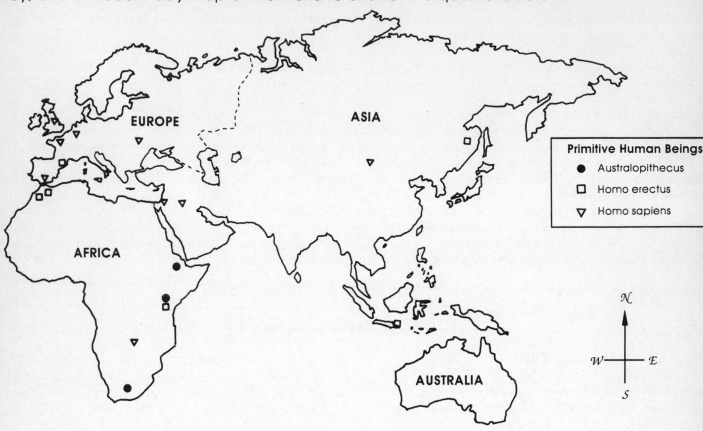

1. This map shows remains from the period of history known as the _____ .

2. Name the continents shown on the map. _____

_____

3. _____ is the only continent where no sites were found.

4. Mainly the remains of Homo _____ are in Europe.

5. How many sites of human remains were found in Africa? _____

6. Remains from which groups were found in China?_____

7. The remains of Homo _____ were found on an island northwest of Australia.

8. The remains of which group were found on the very southern tip of Africa?

_____

9. What body of water is on the east coast of Africa?_____

10. Draw a circle around each Homo sapien site in red.

11. Place a large X on each Homo erectus site in blue.

12. Draw a square around each Australopithecus site in yellow.

Paleolithic Age

Name _____

This map shows the area once inhabited by Stone Age people in parts of Europe, Asia, and Northern Africa. It also shows the types of tools people in these areas made and used. Use this map and a modern map to answer the questions.

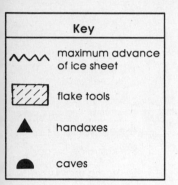

Key

~~	maximum advance of ice sheet
///	flake tools
▲	handaxes
◖	caves

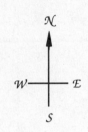

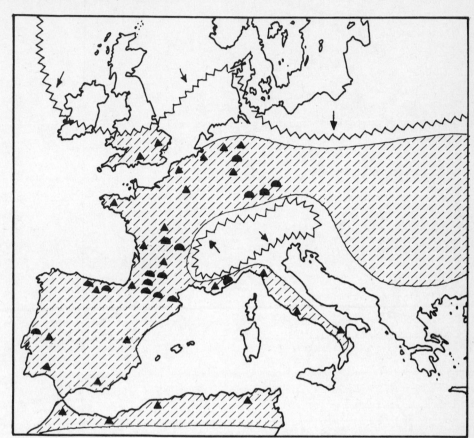

1. Some of the early people lived in caves. What symbol on the map shows the location of caves? _____

2. Did the ice sheet extend into England? _____

3. What does the symbol ▲ stand for on the map? _____

4. The area covered by diagonal lines shows the location where _____ were used.

5. Have any caves been found in central Italy? _____

6. Sites showing evidence of _____ and _____ were located in northern Africa.

7. Name the two types of tools found in Spain and Portugal. _____

   _____

8. Use a blue crayon to color the area covered by the ice sheet.

9. Label the three continents shown on the map.

10. Label the Mediterranean Sea, North Sea, Baltic Sea, and Atlantic Ocean.

Primitive People and Their Art

Name _____

Use this map, the time line, and a modern map of the world to answer the questions.

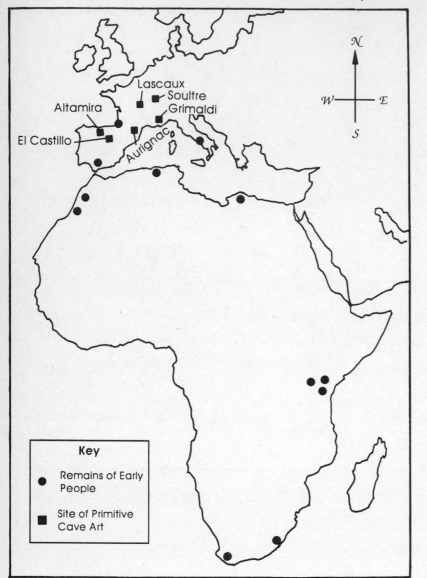

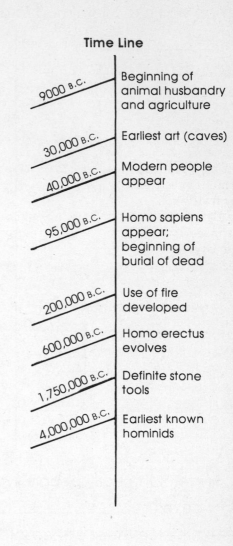

Time Line

9000 B.C.	Beginning of animal husbandry and agriculture
30,000 B.C.	Earliest art (caves)
40,000 B.C.	Modern people appear
95,000 B.C.	Homo sapiens appear; beginning of burial of dead
200,000 B.C.	Use of fire developed
600,000 B.C.	Homo erectus evolves
1,750,000 B.C.	Definite stone tools
4,000,000 B.C.	Earliest known hominids

1. Are the dates on the time line B.C. or A.D.? _____

2. Name the locations where primitive cave art was found. _____

_____

3. Remains of early people were found in how many different places in Africa?_____

4. In what year did people begin to use fire? _____

5. In what year did hominids first appear? _____

6. People first began to draw pictures on cave walls in what year? _____

7. In what year did people begin to make and use stone tools?_____

8. _____ appeared in the year 600,000 B.C.

9. People began to cultivate crops in _____

Ancient Egypt and Mesopotamia

Concept: The first permanent cities in history were located in southwest Asia and northeast Africa.

Objective: Students should understand that people began to live in permanent cities for safety and to gain access to more goods.

Vocabulary: Mesopotamia, Fertile Crescent, pyramid, tomb

Background Information:
- Once people learned to grow their own food, they no longer had to constantly move.
- Mesopotamia grew up along the Tigris and Euphrates rivers. The Greeks named the area Mesopotamia because the name means "between rivers."
- The Fertile Crescent was a crescent-shaped region in Asia that began at the Mediterranean Sea, stretched between the Tigris and Euphrates rivers, and ended at the Persian Gulf.
- Writing was invented by people in Mesopotamia.
- Permanent settlements grew in Egypt along the Nile River. The floodwaters from the Nile provided water and very fertile soil.
- The Egyptians built large stone tombs, called pyramids, as burial places for their rulers.
- Our modern calendar is based on the Egyptian calendar. Their calendar was based on the annual flooding of the Nile River.
- Hieroglyphics, a type of picture writing, was invented by the Egyptians.

Teaching Suggestions

1. Before passing out *Permanent Cities*, point out the area of the world called the Middle East on a large map. This area is also called the Near East. Permanent cities grew here because of the Nile, Tigris, and Euphrates rivers. The land around the rivers is very fertile. The students will need a ruler to complete this activity page.

2. The activity page *Fertile Crescent* highlights the area of southwest Asia called Mesopotamia. Ask students why they think agricultural settlements grew in this area. They should mention the following: fertile soil, water for drinking and irrigation, and ease of travel on the water. Students will need to have a modern map of the region for comparison with the map on the activity page.

3. *Ancient Egypt* shows northeastern Africa. Cities grew up here along the Nile River. This area provided water, rich soil, and valuable minerals. The map includes the location of some pyramids.

Additional Activities

1. Use the code below to help your students understand hieroglyphics or "picture-writing." Write several sentences for the students to decode and then have the students use the code to make up a story for other students to decode.

2. Have the students complete a labeled diagram of the inside of a pyramid.

3. Have the students find at least one important fact about each of these Egyptians: Menes, Thutmose III, Akhenaton, Tutankhamen, Ramses II, and Cleopatra.

A	B	C	D	E	F	G	H	I	J	K	L	M
N	O	P	Q	R	S	T	U	V	W	X	Y	Z

Permanent Cities

Name _____

Use this map and a ruler to answer the questions.

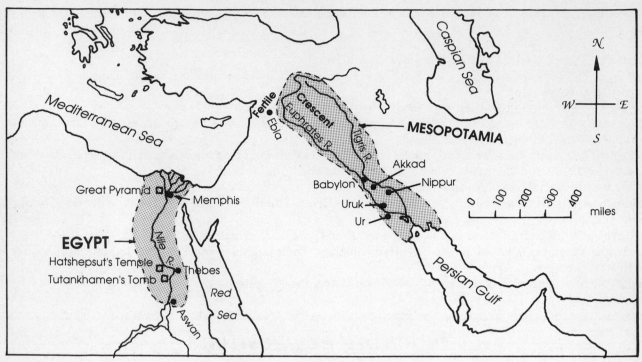

1. Mesopotamia was bordered on the south by which body of water? _____

2. Name the two rivers which helped form the Fertile Crescent. _____

   _____

3. The city of Memphis was located on the banks of the _____ River.

4. Name the three seas shown on the map. _____

   _____

5. _____ tomb was northwest of Aswan.

6 In which direction was the Great Pyramid from Memphis?_____

7. Name the city east of Hatshepsut's Temple. _____

8. Name the river which flows through Egypt. _____

9. Name the area – either Egypt or Mesopotamia – where each city was located.

   A. Babylon _____   D. Aswan _____

   B. Ur _____   E. Akkad _____

   C. Thebes _____

10. Use a ruler and the scale to measure these approximate distances in miles.

   A. Babylon to Ur _____   D. Aswan to Uruk _____

   B. Ebla to Nippur _____   E. Memphis to Aswan _____

   C. Thebes to Ur _____   F. Babylon to Memphis _____

Fertile Crescent

Name _____

Use this map and a modern map of the world to answer the questions.

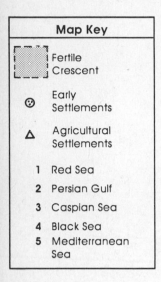

Map Key

⬚ Fertile Crescent

⊗ Early Settlements

△ Agricultural Settlements

1 Red Sea
2 Persian Gulf
3 Caspian Sea
4 Black Sea
5 Mediterranean Sea

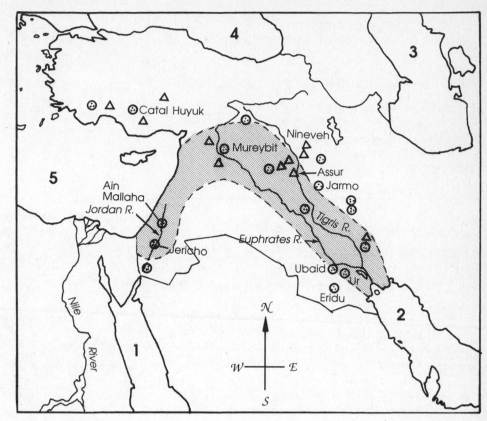

1. The area enclosed by broken lines was called the _____.

2. What symbol shows the location of agricultural settlements? _____

3. Name the two rivers that ran almost the whole length of the Fertile Crescent.

_____

4. Jericho was located near the _____ River.

5. In the blank beside each location, place an **E** for early settlement or an **A** for agricultural settlement.

   A. Jericho _____   C. Mureybit _____   E. Jarmo _____   G. Ubaid _____

   B. Ur _____   D. Assur _____   F. Nineveh _____

6. Identify each numbered body of water on the map.

   1. _____   4. _____

   2. _____   5. _____

   3. _____

7. Use a blue crayon to trace the routes of all four rivers on the map.

8. On the map, label each of the numbered bodies of water.

9. Outline the Fertile Crescent with a red crayon.

Ancient Egypt

Name _____

Use this map to answer the questions below.

1. The _____ River flowed through the center of Ancient Egypt.

2. Were the pyramids located north or south of the Mediterranean Sea?_____

3. Name the three minerals found in the Sinai region. _____ _____

4. What mineral was found between Beni Hasan and Tasa?_____

5. Emeralds were found on the banks of the _____ Sea.

6. _____ was found east of Korosko.

7. _____ was found in four locations close to Kom Ombo.

8. There was a _____ deposit between Heliopolis and Memphis.

9. There are _____ pyramids on the map.

10. Gold was found in _____ different sites.

11. Write the correct letter — **E** or **W** — to tell whether these cities were on the eastern or western side of the Nile River.

A. Anibe _____   E. Thebes _____

B. Buhen _____   F. Tasa _____

C. Kummeh _____   G. Gerzeh _____

D. Serra _____   H. Amrah _____

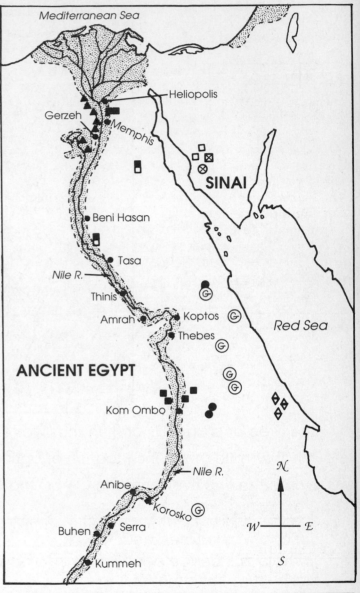

Map Key

▦ Area of Cultivation	▮	Alabaster
▲ Pyramids	▰	Limestone
Ⓖ Gold	☐	Copper
◈ Emerald	⊠	Turquoise
● Granite	⊗	Garnet
■ Sandstone		

Early Civilizations in the Near East

Concept: Three civilizations — Palestine, Persia, and Phoenicia — grew in the region known as the Near East.

Objective: Civilizations flourished in the Near East because of its geographic advantages.

Vocabulary: Near East, civilization, tribe, influence

Background Information:
- Europeans referred to the lands of southwest Asia and part of northeastern Africa as the Near East. The land is southeast of Europe, but closer than China and Japan, which they called the Far East.
- Three continents — Asia, Africa, and Europe — meet in the Near East. It was possible to use land routes to travel from this area to Persia, India, and on to China. Sea routes allowed access to the Indian Ocean and then to the Atlantic and Pacific Oceans.
- The strategic location of the Near East made this region receptive to new ideas brought in by trade, migration, or conquest. Domestication of animals and farming helped the three civilizations to grow and prosper.
- The twelve tribes of Israel, coming from Egypt, settled in the Near East area. By about 1020 B.C., the twelve tribes were under the rule of King Saul.
- The Persian Empire grew up on the land east and west of the Euphrates River. Kings Cyrus, Darius I, and Cambyses extended the empire. In about 500 B.C., the Persian Empire stretched from the Indus River over to northeastern Africa and Greece.
- The Phoenicians occupied a narrow, fertile plain between the Mediterranean Sea and the Lebanon mountain range. Because of its location, many natural resources, and the access to the sea, this land produced many rich merchants. For about 2,000 years, Phoenicia was the center of Mediterranean trade.
- The idea of an alphabet was brought into Phoenicia by traders from the south. In Phoenicia, the alphabet consisted of 22 consonant signs. This alphabet spread to the Hebrews and Romans and from them to the western world.

Teaching Suggestions

1. The students will need a ruler for the activity page *Twelve Tribes of Israel*. Explain to the students that the twelve tribes of Israel were Hebrews organized into 12 groups. Moses led these Israelites out of slavery in Egypt to Canaan (Palestine).

2. For *Growth of the Persian Empire*, students will need a modern map to identify the bodies of water. Point out the size of Persia today. It was a land that included parts of what are now Iran and Afghanistan.

3. Provide the students with modern political maps of Europe, Asia, and northern Africa for activity page *Phoenician Settlements*. Iberia is now divided into two nations — Spain and Portugal.

Additional Activities

1. Have the students construct a wordsearch using terms from this chapter. Example: Persia, Palestine, Israelite, Phoenicia, alphabet, Cyrus, Darius, empire, merchant, etc.

2. Animals were subjects favored by Persian artists. Have each student create an animal drawing to represent your state or city. These drawings could be displayed on the bulletin board.

3. On a chart, have students show an example of the following alphabets: Greek, Gaelic, Hindi, Russian, and Arabic.

Twelve Tribes of Israel

Name _____

Use with page 21.

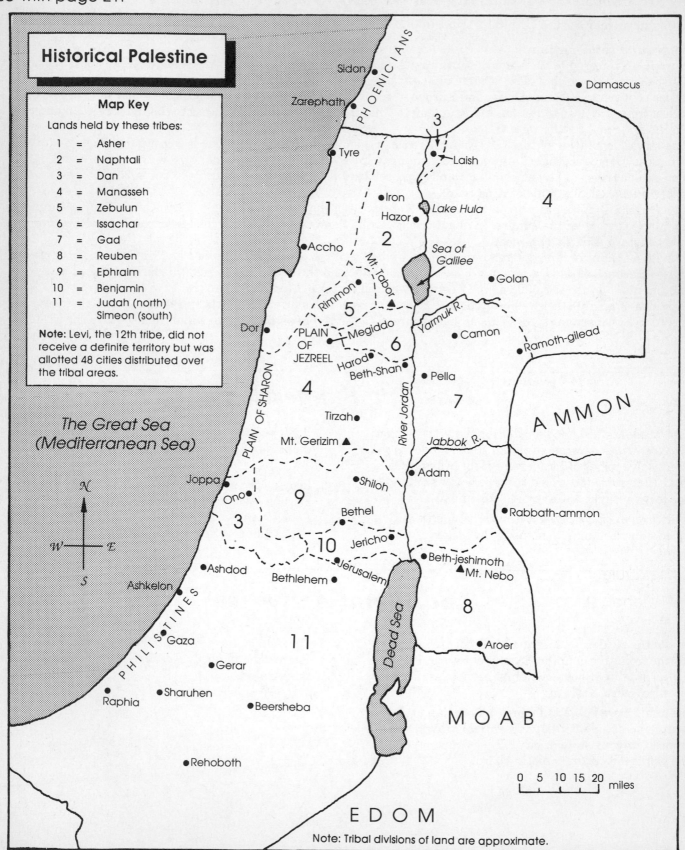

Historical Palestine

Map Key

Lands held by these tribes:

1 = Asher
2 = Naphtali
3 = Dan
4 = Manasseh
5 = Zebulun
6 = Issachar
7 = Gad
8 = Reuben
9 = Ephraim
10 = Benjamin
11 = Judah (north)
Simeon (south)

Note: Levi, the 12th tribe, did not receive a definite territory but was allotted 48 cities distributed over the tribal areas.

The Great Sea (Mediterranean Sea)

Note: Tribal divisions of land are approximate.

Twelve Tribes of Israel (Continued)

Name _____

Use the map on page 20 to answer the questions below.

1. Palestine's western boundary was formed by the _____ Sea, also called the _____ Sea.

2. The tribal land east of the Dead Sea was controlled by the _____ tribe.

3. Which tribe was scattered among 48 cities? _____

4. Tyre and Accho were in an area controlled by the _____ tribe.

5. The Plain of Sharon was on the _____ coast of Palestine.

6. Jericho and Jerusalem were on land occupied by the tribe of _____ .

7. Name the river which flowed between the Dead Sea and the Sea of Galilee.
   _____

8. The city of _____ was southwest of Lake Hula.

9. Which two tribes each occupied two separate areas of land? _____
   _____

10. Mt. Nebo was in the area controlled by the tribe of _____ .

11. Sidon was a city on land held by the _____ .

12. Mt. Gerizim was south of the city of _____ .

13. Other than the Jordan, what two rivers are shown on the map? _____
    _____

14. The city of Joppa was on the banks of the _____ Sea.

15. Laish was located on land held by the tribe of _____ .

16. Use a ruler to measure the approximate distance between these cities.

    A. Rehoboth to Ono _____   F. Hazor to Jericho _____

    B. Damascus to Laish _____   G. Beersheba to Bethlehem _____

    C. Gaza to Joppa _____   H. Aroer to Rimmon _____

    D. Jericho to Golan _____   I. Dor to Adam _____

    E. Shiloh to Beth-Shan _____   J. Ashdod to Tyre _____

Growth of the Persian Empire

Name _____

Use this map and a map of the Persian Empire to answer the questions.

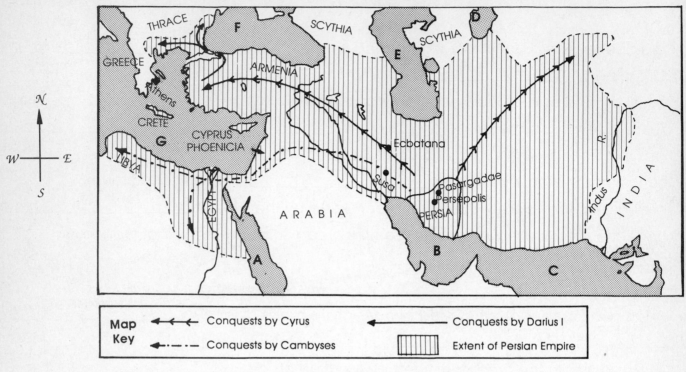

1. _____ was located outside the Persian Empire, by the Black and Caspian seas.

2. Did the Persian Empire cross the Indus River? _____

3. Name the two cities located in Persia. _____

4. Which ruler conquered Egypt and Libya? _____

5. Name the ruler whose routes went both northeast and northwest from Persia.

_____

6. Name the land located between Persia and Egypt. _____

7. According to the map on this page, _____ was the first city Cyrus reached on his northwest route from Persia.

8. Name the first city Cambyses reached after he left Persia, according to the map on this page. _____

9. Name the ruler whose route took him into Greece. _____

10. Identify the bodies of water indicated on the map with the following letters.

A. _____   E. _____

B. _____   F. _____

C. _____   G. _____

D. _____

Phoenician Settlements

Name _____

This map shows the extent of Phoenician influence between the 8th and the 6th centuries B.C. It also shows a few of the many items traded by the Phoenicians. Answer the questions below.

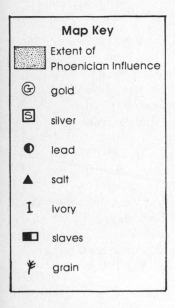

Map Key

- Extent of Phoenician Influence
- Ⓖ gold
- Ⓢ silver
- ◑ lead
- ▲ salt
- I ivory
- ◼ slaves
- ⚥ grain

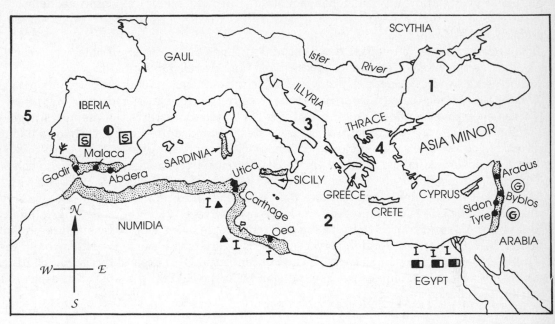

1. The _____ River separated Scythia from Illyria.

2. Name the two products used for trade found southwest of Carthage. _____
_____

3. Which two products were found in Egypt? _____

4. Name the island off the southern coast of Greece. _____

5. _____ was the product found near Aradus and Byblos. _____

6. Which of these islands had Phoenician settlements — **Crete** or **Cyprus**? _____

7. _____ , _____ , and _____ were the three products found in Iberia.

8. Gadir was located on the southern coast of _____ .

9. Identify the bodies of water indicated on the map with the following numbers.

   1. _____   4. _____

   2. _____   5. _____

   3. _____

Ancient Greece

Concept: The ancient Greeks had a profound influence on the shaping of our world. They were the first to live in a democracy and were the founders of western civilization.

Objective: To help students understand that Greece is the birthplace of many customs and ideologies important to our society today.

Vocabulary: city-state, citizen, dependent state, allied state, empire, longitude, democracy

Background Information:
- The ancient Greeks carried on trade with many lands, near and far. Trade was accomplished by traveling across the sea, as the rugged terrain in Greece made land travel very difficult.
- The Greeks lived in or near city-states. Each city-state was independent with its own government and laws. Citizens and noncitizens (slaves and serfs) lived in the city-states. However, not all citizens were equal. Some citizens had more power than others. It was from these city-states that democratic government began.
- Athens and Sparta were the greatest city-states in ancient Greece. Sparta's laws had one main purpose: to produce good soldiers. The majority of Athens' citizens were traders.
- Greece's power came to an end when the city-states started waging war against each other. In 338 B.C., King Philip II of Macedonia conquered all of the city-states except Sparta. At Philip's death, his son, Alexander, carried out his father's plans to make war on the Persian Empire.
- Alexander the Great conquered all the lands from Greece to the Indus River located in what we know today as Pakistan. Alexander tried to unite the different people in his empire by encouraging intermarriages. To set an example, he married a Persian princess. He brought Greek ideas and customs to all the countries he conquered.
- Greek colonization began as early as the 8th century B.C. to expand territorial holdings, decrease land hunger, and increase trade. Colonies were founded in northern Greece, the Black Sea area, and in what is now Italy, Sicily, and northern Africa.

Teaching Suggestions

1. Share the information on city-states found in the **Background Information** above with the students. The activity page *Greek City-States* asks the students to read a map, use a scale to measure distance, and use simple division to answer the questions. It would be helpful if you show the students this area on a map of the world or on a globe before they are given the activity sheet. Explain to them that the activity page contains a map of ancient Greece, showing where many of the city-states were once located.

2. On the activity page *Settlements of Ancient Greece,* be sure students understand that the dates on the map are B.C. Remind the class that B.C. dates decrease the closer they come to A.D. You may want to help students with question number 2 since it may be difficult for many of them.

3. Prior to passing out the activity page *The Athenian Empire,* explain the difference between a Greek allied state and dependent state to the class. (See glossary for definitions.)

4. Before giving students the activity page *Alexander's Conquests: 336-323 B.C.,* go over the information on Alexander the Great under **Background Information.** The students must use the map, map key, and the table to answer the questions.

5. Students will need a modern map for the activity page *Alexander the Great's Empire.* Remind them that the answers to number 3 must include the number, degree symbol (°), and direction to be correct.

Additional Activities

1. Tell students the legend of the wooden horse the Greeks used to defeat the city of Troy. The legend is described simply in *World Book Encyclopedia* under "Troy." Have students devise another surprise weapon the Greeks could have used.

2. Homer, a blind Greek poet, told how the gods and goddesses involved themselves in the lives of the Athenians. Let the students write stories or poems about a modern-day god or goddess who might help their families.

Greek City-States

Name _____

This map of ancient Greece shows the location of many of the Greek city-states. Use this map and a ruler to answer the questions.

1. Name the four seas shown on the map. _____

   _____

2. Lindus was on the island of _____ .

3. Name three city-states found on the island of Crete. _____

   _____

4. Was Sparta in southern or northern Greece? _____

5. The large land area east of the Aegean Sea was called _____ .

6. Name the mountain located in Thessaly. _____

7. Halicarnassus is northwest of the island of _____ .

8. About how far is it from the western coast of Crete to the eastern coast? _____

9. Use a ruler to measure the approximate distances between the following cities.

   A. Sparta to Thebes _____   C. Samos to Miletus _____

   B. Cydonia to Itanos _____   D. Byzantium to Miletus _____

10. Walking 25 miles a day, about how many days would it take you to walk from:

   A. Calchedo to Miletus _____   C. Sparta to Thebes _____

   B. Sparta to Argos _____   D. Colophon to Abydos _____

Settlements of Ancient Greece

Name _____

Use this map to answer the questions.

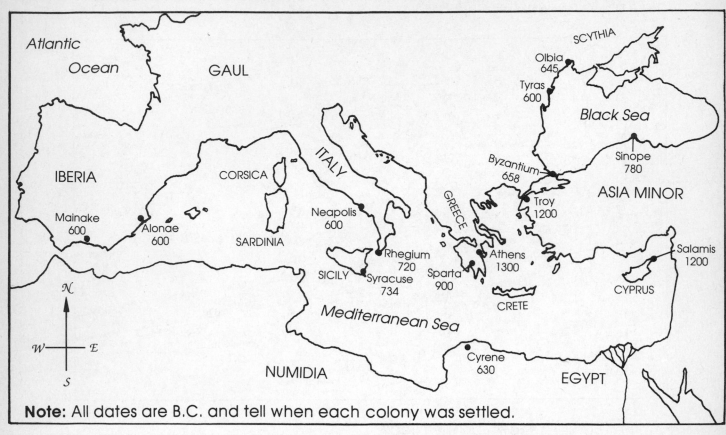

Note: All dates are B.C. and tell when each colony was settled.

1. For each settlement below, name the country and/or island on which it is located.

   A. Salamis _____   E. Syracuse _____

   B. Alonae _____   F. Neapolis _____

   C. Olbia _____   G. Rhegium _____

   D. Athens _____   H. Mainake _____

2. Write the years these places were settled in the blanks. Then rank the settlements below from 1 – 8 with number one being the oldest settlement and number eight being the most recent.

	Year	Rank		Date	Rank
A. Neapolis	_____	_____	E. Cyrene	_____	_____
B. Rhegium	_____	_____	F. Syracuse	_____	_____
C. Athens	_____	_____	G. Byzantium	_____	_____
D. Salamis	_____	_____	H. Sparta	_____	_____

The Athenian Empire

Name _____

Use this map and a ruler to answer the questions.

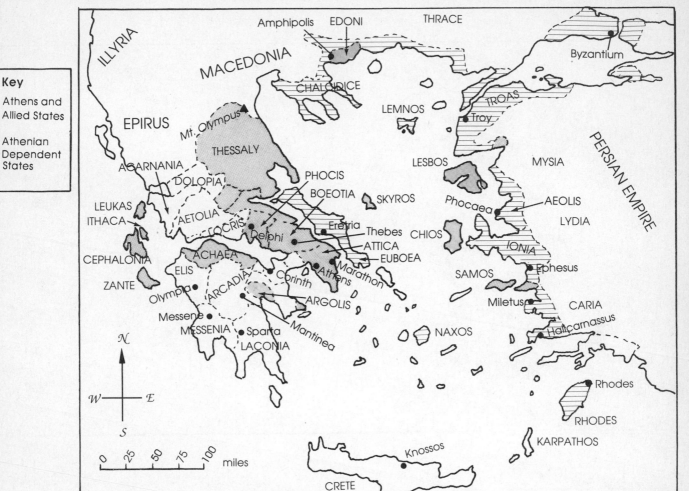

1. Tell whether these locations were allied states (A) or dependent states (D) by writing the correct letter in the blank.

   A. Cephalonia _____   F. Achaea _____

   B. Attica _____   G. Troas _____

   C. Thessaly _____   H. Ithaca _____

   D. Rhodes _____   I. Naxos _____

   E. Euboea _____   J. Ionia _____

2. Use a ruler to measure the approximate distance between these cities or places.

   A. Ephesus to Halicarnassus _____   E. Messene to Knossos _____

   B. Athens to Sparta _____   F. Delphi to Marathon _____

   C. Mt. Olympus to Byzantium _____   G. Corinth to Sparta _____

   D. Troy to Eretria _____   H. Phocaea to Rhodes _____

3. Outline Athens and the allied states with a yellow crayon.

Alexander's Conquests: 336-323 B.C.

Name _____

Use with page 29.

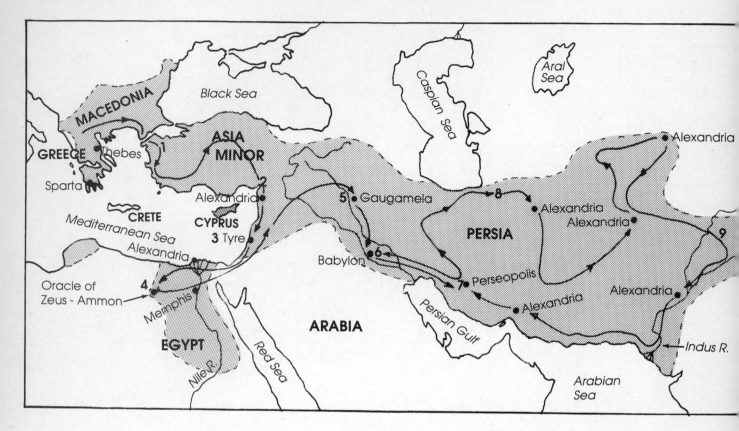

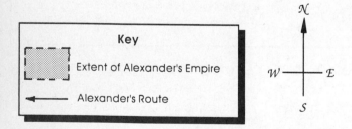

Key

Extent of Alexander's Empire

Alexander's Route

Major Events and Battles During Alexander's Conquests

1. Battle at Granicus River 334 B.C.

2. Battle of Issus 333 B.C.

3. Alexander captured Tyre 332 B.C.

4. Alexander visited oracle of Zeus–Ammon 331 B.C.

5. Alexander defeated King Darius III of Persia at Gaugamela 331 B.C.

6. Alexander established capital at Babylon 331 B.C. (He died at Babylon in 323 B.C.)

7. Alexander burned Persepolis in 330 B.C.

8. Alexander and his army entered the heartland of Persia in 330 B.C.

9. Alexander defeated Indian Prince Porus in 326 B.C.

Alexander's Conquests: 336-323 B.C.

(Continued)   Name _____

Use the map and the information on page 28 to answer the questions here.

1. Was the island of Cyprus part of Alexander's empire? _____

2. What did Alexander do in Egypt? _____

3. Why do you think there are so many cities named Alexandria on the map? _____
_____

4. After Alexander defeated King Darius III at Gaugámela, did Alexander go on to Tyre or

   Babylon? _____

5. Was Sparta, Greece, part of Alexander's empire? _____

6. Macedonia's eastern boundary was the _____ Sea.

7. In the year _____ , Alexander and his army entered the heartland of Persia.

8. The city of Memphis was in the country of _____ .

9. The island of _____ is southeast of Greece.

10. The land between the Mediterranean Sea and the Black Sea was called
    _____ .

11. The _____ Gulf is south of Persia.

12. What city did Alexander burn in 330 B.C.? _____

13. The Battle of _____ was in the year 333 B.C.

14. In what year did Alexander establish a capital at Babylon? _____

15. Number these events in chronological order with the earliest event being number one.
    (The first one has been done for you.) You may wish to write the year next to each
    event before beginning.

    A. _____ Alexander defeated Prince Porus.

    B. _____ Alexander entered the heartland of Persia.

    C. _____ Alexander captured Tyre.

    D. _____ Battle of Issus

    E. _____ Alexander died at Babylon.

    F. _____ Alexander defeated King Darius III.

    G. ___1___ Battle at Granicus River

Alexander the Great's Empire

Name _____

Use this map and a modern map to answer the questions below.

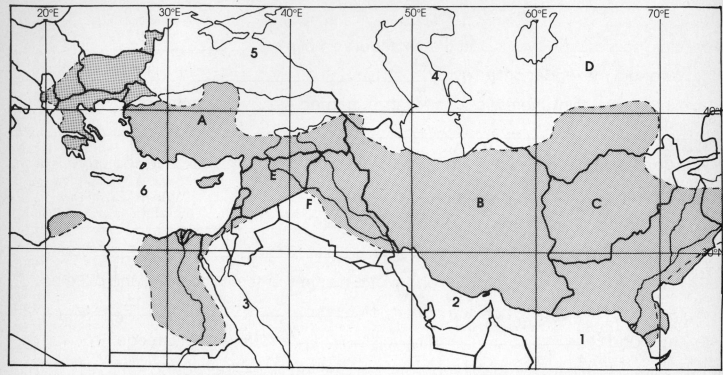

Map Key

▨ Extent of Alexander's Empire —— Modern boundaries between countries

1. Write the correct number of each body of water beside its name.

_____ Arabian Sea   _____ Mediterranean Sea   _____ Red Sea

_____ Caspian Sea   _____ Persian Gulf   _____ Black Sea

2. Write the modern name of each country beside its matching letter.

A. _____   D. _____

B. _____   E. _____

C. _____   F. _____

3. Which line(s) of longitude pass through these places?

A. Iran _____   D. Afghanistan _____

B. Turkey _____   E. Caspian Sea _____

C. Iraq _____   F. Persian Gulf _____

4. Use a green crayon to lightly color in Alexander's empire.

Roman Empire

Concept: The ancient Romans helped shape Western civilization in the areas of government, art, and architecture. Their influence can still be seen throughout our world today.

Objective: The languages, political systems, and calendars of many countries today are directly related to ancient Rome.

Vocabulary: republic, aqueduct, sewer, Latin, peninsula, via, imperial province, senatorial province, dependent state, conquest

Background Information:
- Rome was a republic from 509 to 27 B.C. The Romans were the first to have a government that imposed central authority on big areas while still keeping a local government.
- With the rule of Augustus in 27 B.C., the Roman Empire replaced the Roman Republic. Augustus had supreme authority, and the Roman government became an absolute monarchy. At its peak in the A.D. 100's, the Roman Empire extended into three continents—Europe, Africa, and Asia. It surrounded the Mediterranean Sea.
- The city of Rome grew with the empire. Some historians estimate that one million people lived in or near Rome during the reign of Augustus (27 B.C. – A.D. 14).
- Roman engineers built waterways, called aqueducts, to bring clean water to the city. They also constructed sewers to carry the waste away. The Romans used stone and brick for building. In all parts of their empire, they built cities, roads, bridges, and aqueducts. It is still possible to visit the remains of temples, theaters, baths, and other buildings.
- The extent of Roman influence can be seen in many aspects of our lives today. For instance, we use basically the same calendar that the Romans used. Almost half of the English words used today were borrowed from the Roman language, Latin. Even the law systems of many modern nations are based on Roman law.

Teaching Suggestions

1. Start off this unit by pointing out Italy on a map or a globe. Ask students what type of land form Italy is. (peninsula) Ask them what Italy's shape reminds them of. (boot) Explain to students that the Romans built roads throughout their empire. The activity page *Roman Highways* shows the highways found in Italy. In Italian, a road is called *via*. *Via* is Latin for "way."

2. The Roman Republic ended and the Roman Empire began under Augustus. Augustus ruled for about 40 years. Some writers call his reign the "golden age of Rome." Define the terms imperial province, senatorial province, dependent state, and conquest for the class. (See *glossary*.) Hand out the activity page *Empire of Augustus* (27 B.C. - A.D. 14) now.

3. Use a map of the world in conjunction with the activity page *The Roman Empire117 A.D.*, to show students how large the Roman Empire truly was. Ask students why the size is so amazing. (slow transportation and communication; soldiers and supplies were carried on horseback; poor methods for food preservation, etc.)

Additional Activities

1. Read the story of Romulus and Remus and the founding of Rome to the class. Have them draw cartoon strips based on this story or create a puppet show for younger students.

2. Roman baths were not used just to get clean. Have pairs of students research this subject. On a chart, they can compare and contrast them with modern fitness centers.

3. Gladiators were usually slaves or criminals condemned to death. Fighting in the Colosseum gave them a chance to live. Have the students research this type of capital punishment. Use the following question for a debate: "Was Roman punishment more or less fair than what we use today?"

Roman Highways

Name _____

Use this map and a ruler to answer the questions.

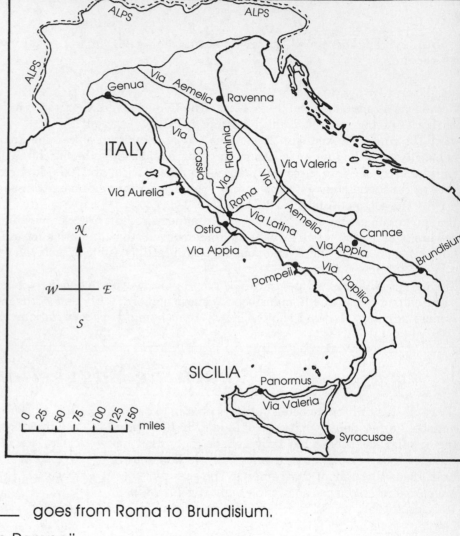

1. Name the mountains north of Italy.

   _____

2. The island of

   _____

   is southwest of Italy.

3. The *Via* _____ goes from Roma to Brundisium.

4. Name the *via* which goes to Pompeii. _____

5. The *Via* _____ is the only highway on Sicilia.

6. The *Via* _____ travels along the western coast to the north.

7. Use a ruler to measure the approximate distances between these cities.

   A. Roma to Pompeii   _____   D. Genua to Ostia   _____

   B. Panormus to Syracusae _____   E. Ravenna to Cannae _____

   C. Cannae to Brundisium _____

8. Trace these routes:

   A. Via Aemelia with a red crayon.   C. Via Flaminia with a green crayon.

   B. Via Latina with a yellow crayon.   D. Via Appia with a blue crayon.

Empire of Augustus (27 B.C. - A.D. 14)

Name _____

Use the map below to answer the questions.

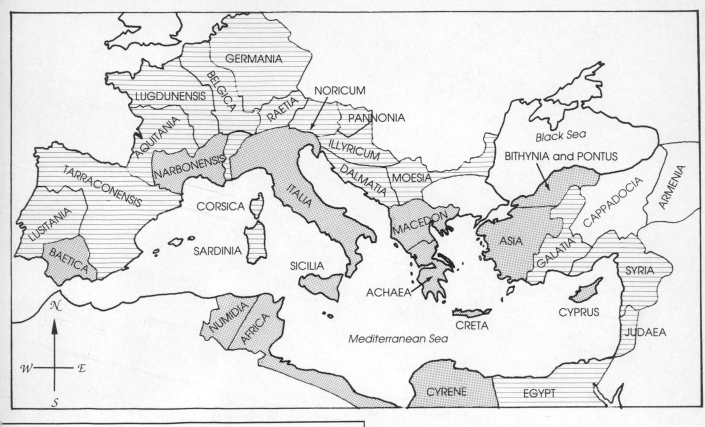

Key

Imperial provinces   Senatorial provinces

1. Write the correct letter in the blank to show whether the areas below were imperial provinces (**I**) or senatorial provinces (**S**).

A. _____ Aquitania   E. _____ Lusitania   I. _____ Dalmatia

B. _____ Baetica   F. _____ Syria   J. _____ Cyrene

C. _____ Macedon   G. _____ Numidia

D. _____ Asia   H. _____ Pannonia

2. Is Germania north or south of Italia? _____

3. Which Mediterranean islands were senatorial provinces? _____

_____

4. Which Mediterranean islands were imperial provinces? _____

_____

5. Is Egypt west or east of Cyrene? _____

The Roman Empire A.D. 117

Name _____

Use this map to answer the questions.

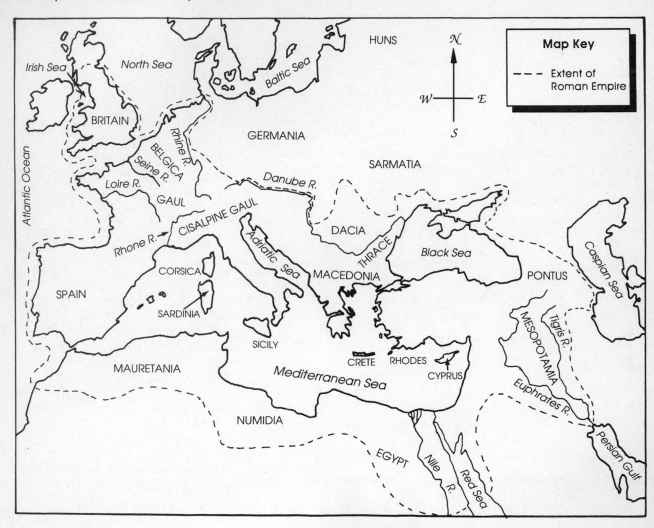

1. What does the broken line show? _____

2. Did the Roman Empire extend north of the Black Sea? _____

3. The _____ River separated Belgica from Germania.

4. Name the sea north of Germania. _____

5. Which two rivers flow into the Persian Gulf? _____

6. Name the six islands in the Mediterranean Sea. _____

_____

7. The Roman Empire extended east to the _____ Sea.

8. The Loire River is in _____ .

9. Was Britain part of the Roman Empire? _____

10. Use a yellow crayon to outline the Roman Empire.

Europe in the Middle Ages

Concept: The early Middle Ages in Europe saw the fall of Rome and the establishment of barbarian kingdoms on the continent.

Objective: Between the years A.D. 180 and A.D. 800, the Roman Empire fell and barbarians invaded Europe.

Vocabulary: barbarian, kingdom, clan, artisan, tribute

Background Information:
- Nature gave Europe a favorable climate, navigable rivers, mountains, rich soil, and a variety of minerals.
- Germanic tribes (or Germanic kingdoms) like the Angles, Franks, Jutes, Saxons, Vandals, and Visigoths were living in northern Europe at the time of the Roman Empire. They lived in tribes governed by a chief. The economy was based on a crude type of farming and hunting. Some trade was carried on between the Germans and people in the Mediterranean area.
- The Huns affected the history of Europe for over 80 years. They invaded Europe from Asia and wanted to dominate others.
- The Slavs invaded Europe from Asia. These people had highly developed agricultural and horticultural systems. The communities in which they lived were self-contained. Spinning and weaving were their main domestic industries. In general, the Slavs lived in peace with the Romans.
- During the 4th and 5th centuries, barbarians invaded Europe. Angles, Saxons, and Jutes invaded Britain. The Franks moved into Gaul, and Spain was invaded by the Vandals. The Visigoths and Ostrogoths imposed their rule on Italy. These groups established kingdoms known as early Germanic states.
- The Franks became the most powerful political force in Europe in the Middle Ages. Charlemagne, one of the most famous rulers of the Middle Ages, became ruler of all the Franks in A.D. 771. For the rest of his reign, he tried to impose his power on all the people of Europe.

Teaching Suggestions

1. *Barbarian Invaders* and *Europe in A.D. 400* show the extent of the Western and Eastern Roman Empires in the early Middle Ages. Putting a time line of the barbarian invasions on the chalkboard might help some students. Use either activity at this time.

2. Students will need a modern map to identify the bodies of water on the map on the activity page *Germanic States A.D. 526.* Be sure you have gone over the information concerning the Germanic tribes (kingdoms) in the **Background Information** before passing out this activity.

3. *England A.D. 800* shows the division of England by the Angles, Saxons, and Jutes. Locate England on a modern map to point out its close proximity to the rest of Europe.

4. Despite years of war and his vast empire, Charlemagne never controlled the entire continent. He was, however, responsible for many positive changes in his empire. Use *Charlemagne's Empire A.D. 800* now.

Additional Activities

1. Have students research the art of tapestry making. In the past, the designs on tapestries often depicted an event in a family or area. Let the students create a tapestry design depicting an event from their own lives.

2. Coats of arms were once used to identify different knights on a battlefield. They were used to decorate shields, banners, furniture, flags, and other possessions. Symbols were used to represent important things to the knight. Have students design a coat of arms for a famous person. Additional information on coats of arms may be found in an encyclopedia under "Heraldry."

Barbarian Invaders

Name _____

Use the map below to answer the questions and learn about Europe during the time of barbarian invasions.

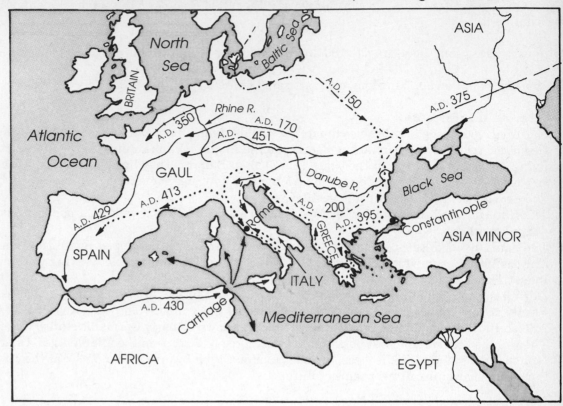

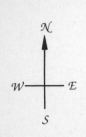

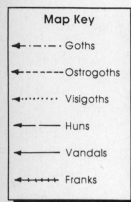

Map Key

◄–·–·– Goths

◄–––– Ostrogoths

◄·········· Visigoths

◄–––– Huns

◄––––– Vandals

◄–++++– Franks

1. The Huns came from the continent of _____ .

2. The Vandals moved in five different directions from the city of _____ .

3. The Franks crossed the _____ River to invade Gaul.

4. Name the two groups which invaded Italy._____

5. The Goths crossed the _____ Sea in A.D. 150.

6. The Visigoths left Italy to invade which two regions?_____

7. The Vandals crossed the Rhine River in the year_____ .

8. In what year did the Huns invade Gaul?_____

9. The _____ crossed the Danube River in A.D. 395.

10. Name the group which invaded Greece. _____

11. The Vandals invaded the city of _____ in A.D. 430.

12. Rank these events in order beginning with the earliest event. **(Hint: First write the years next to the events.)**

_____ A. Huns enter Gaul.   _____ D. Ostrogoths enter Italy.

_____ B. Franks enter Gaul   _____ E. Vandals enter Spain.

_____ C. Vandals enter Gaul.   _____ F. Visigoths enter Spain.

Europe in A.D. 400

Name _____

Use the map below to answer the questions.

Map Key

Eastern Roman Empire

Western Roman Empire

1. Place a **W** (Western Roman Empire) or an **E** (Eastern Roman Empire) in the blank to show the correct empire for each place.

_____ A. Egypt   _____ E. Gaul

_____ B. Italy   _____ F. Mauretania

_____ C. Britain   _____ G. Asia Minor

_____ D. Greece   _____ H. Spain

2. Was Scandia part of either empire? _____

3. The land in Asia north of the Black Sea was occupied by _____ and _____ .

4. The _____ River separated Gaul from Germany.

5. Were the Scots part of the Roman Empire? _____

6. Use a ruler to measure the approximate distance between these cities.

_____ A. Rome to Carthage   _____ D. Toledo to Braga

_____ B. Constantinople to Rome   _____ E. Ravenna to Cartagena

_____ C. Toulouse to Carthage   _____ F. Syracuse to Constantinople

Germanic States A.D. 526

Name _____

Use the map below to answer the questions.

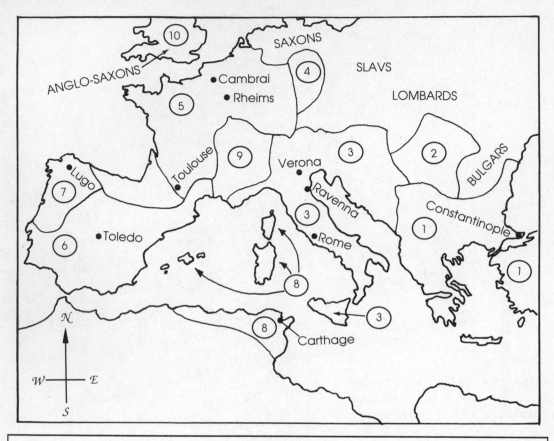

Map Key

① East Roman Empire   ⑤ Kingdom of the Franks   ⑧ Vandal Kingdom
② Gepid Kingdom   ⑥ Kingdom of the Visigoths   ⑨ Burgundian Kingdom
③ Ostrogothic Kingdom   ⑦ Kingdom of the Suevi   ⑩ Anglo-Saxons
④ Thuringian Kingdom

1. For each city below, name the Germanic kingdom it was a part of in A.D. 526.

A. Carthage _____   F. Toulouse _____

B. Rheims _____   G. Lugo _____

C. Rome _____   H. Ravenna _____

D. Toledo _____   I. Cambrai _____

E. Constantinople _____   J. Verona _____

2. Outline each Germanic kingdom with the color named.

A. East Roman Empire — red   E. Franks — green   H. Vandal — black

B. Gepid — light blue   F. Visigoths — yellow   I. Burgundian — pink

C. Ostrogothic — orange   G. Suevi — purple   J. Anglo-Saxons — dark blue

D. Thuringian — brown

England A.D. 800

Name _____

Use the map below to answer the questions.

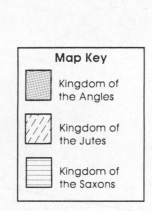

Map Key

Kingdom of the Angles

Kingdom of the Jutes

Kingdom of the Saxons

1. Name the body of water between England and Gaul. _____

_____

2. The North Sea was _____ of England.

3. The _____ Sea was west of England.

4. The Celts occupied which three areas?

_____

_____

5. Northumbria, Mercia, and East Anglia were occupied by the _____ .

6. Wessex, Essex, and Sussex were occupied by the _____ .

7. _____ was the only area occupied by Jutes.

8. The Irish Sea separated _____ from England.

9. For each town below, name the section of England in which it was located.

A. Tamworth _____

B. Durham _____

C. Lincoln _____

D. Canterbury _____

E. Gloucester _____

F. Dunwich _____

G. Winchester _____

H. Edinburgh _____

I. London _____

J. Chichester _____

Charlemagne's Empire A.D. 800

Name _____

Use this map to answer the questions.

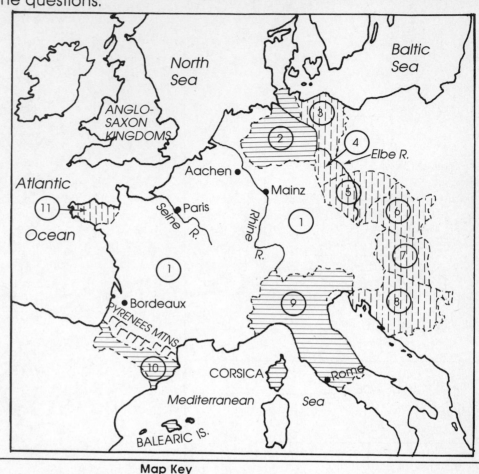

Map Key

① Frankish Kingdom in A.D. 768   ④ Wends   ⑦ Pannonian March   ⑩ Spanish March

② Saxons   ⑤ Bohemians   ⑧ Croats   ⑪ Bretons

③ Wilzi   ⑥ Moravians   ⑨ Lombards

▤ Areas added to Frankish Kingdom by Charlemagne

▥ People who paid tribute to Charlemagne

1. Which mountains formed the southwestern border of the Frankish Kingdom?_____

2. Name five areas and/or tribes Charlemagne conquered and added to the empire

   after A.D. 768. _____

   _____

3. Name the seven groups of people who paid tribute to Charlemagne. _____

   _____

4. The cities of Bordeaux and Paris were part of the _____ Kingdom

5. The city of Mainz is on the _____ River.

6. The city of Paris is on the _____ River.

7. Rome was in an area which was occupied by the _____ .

The Birthplace and Spread of Three Religions

Concept: The Middle East was the birthplace of three of the world's great religions — Judaism, Christianity, and Islam.

Objective: Judaism, Christianity, and Islam began in the Middle East and spread to many parts of the world.

Vocabulary: Middle East, Judaism, Christianity, Islam, Jews, Christians, Moslems, prophet, Crusades, Dead Sea Scrolls

Background Information:
- Three continents—Africa, Asia, and Europe — meet in the Middle East.
- Three of the world's major religions — Judaism, Christianity, and Islam — began in the Middle East. People who believe in these religions are called, respectively, Jews, Christians, and Moslems.
- Judaism is the history of the Israelites. The Israelites lived in the Middle East 3,000-4,000 years ago. They conquered a land known as Canaan, which encompassed pretty much the same land as modern Israel.
- The Christian religion grew out of ancient Judaism. Jesus, the founder of Christianity, was a Jew. A man named Paul traveled throughout Asia Minor and Greece to spread Christianity.
- Moslems believe that Mohammed, the founder of the Islamic religion, was the greatest and last of all God's messengers. His teachings are called Islam, which means "submission." The word Moslem means "one who submits (to God)."
- The crusades were Christian military expeditions organized to recapture the Holy Land from the Moslems. A variety of people joined the crusades including knights, nobles, merchants, and peasants. There were eight crusades, but one of the most tragic was the Children's Crusade. Thousands of young boys and girls, many less than 12 years old, made their way to European seaports. However, none of them ever made it to the Holy Land and few returned home. Many died of hunger and cold, and others were sold to the Moslems as slaves.

Teaching Suggestions

1. The students will need a ruler for the first activity page, *Ancient Israel*. The map on this page shows the land controlled by kings David and Solomon. A large map of the Middle East will be helpful.

2. *Palestine in the First Century* A.D. shows the Middle East as it was during the life of Jesus. It also shows the cave where the Dead Sea Scrolls were discovered.

3. The students will need a modern map of Europe, Asia, and northern Africa to complete the activity page *Spread of Christianity*.

4. Ask the students why Islam did not spread further south than it did. (Africa was a desert with few people.) Before handing out *Expansion of Islam to* A.D. *750*, talk about the Children's Crusade. Explain to students that few of the crusades were successful.

Additional Activities

1. The Dead Sea and the Dead Sea Scrolls are interesting topics for research. Suggested questions for the students to answer: Why is it called the Dead Sea? Why is it almost impossible for a swimmer to sink in the Dead Sea? What is the mineral content of the water? Where were the Dead Sea Scrolls found and who found them? Why are the Scrolls important?

2. Divide the class into groups of 4 or 5 students. Each group should create a puppet show based on one of the stories from the *Arabian Nights*.

3. Have groups of students compare Judaism, Christianity, and Islam. Give them categories to use in their comparisons—i.e., date founded, founded by, main beliefs, days of special celebration, etc.

Ancient Israel

Name _____

Use with page 43.

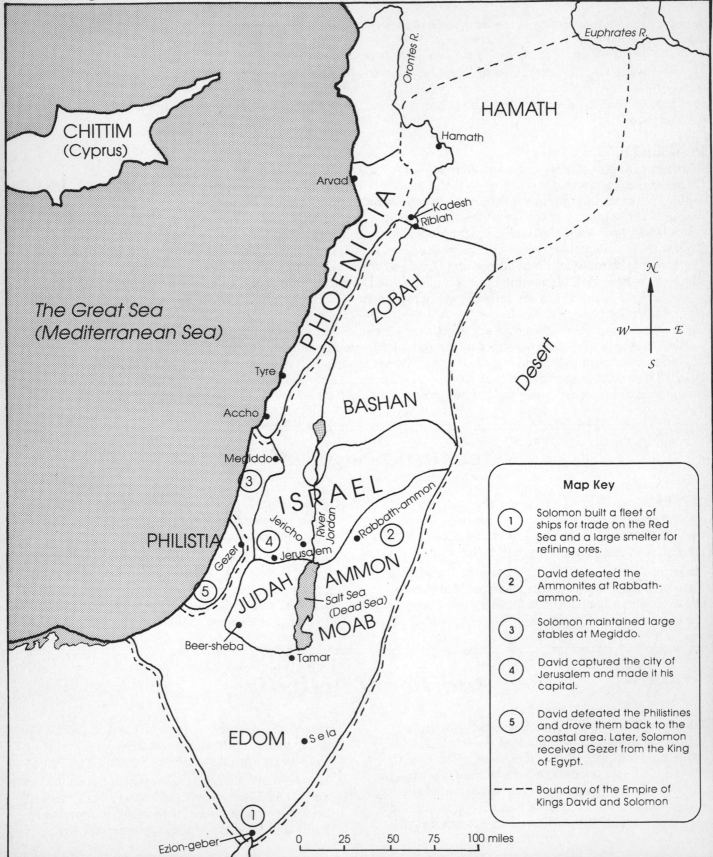

CHITTIM (Cyprus)

HAMATH
• Hamath

Orontes R.
Euphrates R.

Arvad •

• Kadesh
• Riblah

The Great Sea (Mediterranean Sea)

PHOENICIA

ZOBAH

N
W ⊕ E
S

Tyre •

BASHAN

Desert

Accho •

Megiddo •
③

ISRAEL

PHILISTIA

Jericho •
④

River Jordan

• Rabbath-ammon
②

Gezer •
⑤

• Jerusalem

AMMON

JUDAH

Salt Sea (Dead Sea)

• Beer-sheba

MOAB

• Tamar

EDOM   • Sela

Map Key

① Solomon built a fleet of ships for trade on the Red Sea and a large smelter for refining ores.

② David defeated the Ammonites at Rabbath-ammon.

③ Solomon maintained large stables at Megiddo.

④ David captured the city of Jerusalem and made it his capital.

⑤ David defeated the Philistines and drove them back to the coastal area. Later, Solomon received Gezer from the King of Egypt.

– – – Boundary of the Empire of Kings David and Solomon

①
Ezion-geber

0   25   50   75   100 miles

Ancient Israel (Continued)

Name _____

Use the map and key on page 42 and a ruler to answer the questions.

1. The broken line on the map shows the boundary of the empire of

   Kings _____ and _____ .

2. What two things did Solomon build at Ezion-geber? _____

   _____

3. Which king defeated the Ammonites? _____

4. The capital city for David's empire was _____ .

5. Who defeated the Philistines? _____

6. Solomon received the city of Gezer from the King of _____ .

7. Solomon maintained large stables at _____ .

8. At this time in history, Cyprus was known as _____ .

9. What name do we give the Great Sea today? _____

10. Accho and Tyre were on land called _____ .

11. Jericho was located near the River _____ .

12. The _____ River formed the northeastern boundary of David and

    Solomon's empire.

13. The city of Hamath was on the banks of the _____ River.

14. What type of land was east of Israel? _____

15. Use a ruler to measure the distances between these cities.

    A. Tamar to Sela   _____

    B. Megiddo to Beer-sheba   _____

    C. Gezer to Ezion-geber   _____

    D. Arvad to Accho   _____

    E. Hamath to Kadesh   _____

16. Use a red crayon to outline the empire of Kings David and Solomon.

17. Outline the area controlled by Phoenicia with a green crayon.

18. Outline the area known as Philistia with an orange crayon.

19. Trace the route of the River Jordan with a blue crayon.

Palestine in the First Century A.D.

Name _____

Use this map to answer the questions.

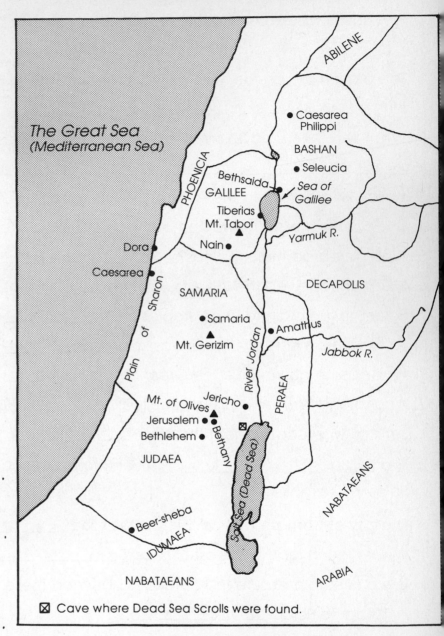

The Great Sea
(Mediterranean Sea)

ABILENE

• Caesarea Philippi

BASHAN

• Seleucia

PHOENICIA

Bethsaida
GALILEE

Sea of Galilee

Tiberias
Mt. Tabor

Nain •

Yarmuk R.

Dora •

DECAPOLIS

Caesarea •

Plain of Sharon

SAMARIA

• Samaria

▲ Mt. Gerizim

• Amathus

Jabbok R.

River Jordan

Mt. of Olives ▲

Jericho •

PERAEA

Jerusalem • •
Bethlehem •

Bethany

JUDAEA

Salt Sea (Dead Sea)

NABATAEANS

Beer-sheba •

IDUMAEA

NABATAEANS

ARABIA

☒ Cave where Dead Sea Scrolls were found.

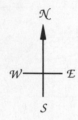

N
W — E
S

1. The Salt Sea is now known as the _____ .

2. Tiberias was on the banks of the _____ .

3. Name the mountain south of the city of Samaria.

_____

4. The Mt. of _____ was located near Jerusalem and Bethany.

5. Mt. Tabor was north of the city of _____ .

6. Name three cities found in Bashan. _____

7. Caesarea was on the Plain of _____ .

8. Amathus was east of the River _____ and north of the _____ River.

9. Dora was on the banks of the _____ Sea.

10. Beer-sheba was in the southern part of _____ .

11. The Dead Sea Scrolls were found in a _____ .

Spread of Christianity

se with page 46.

Name _____

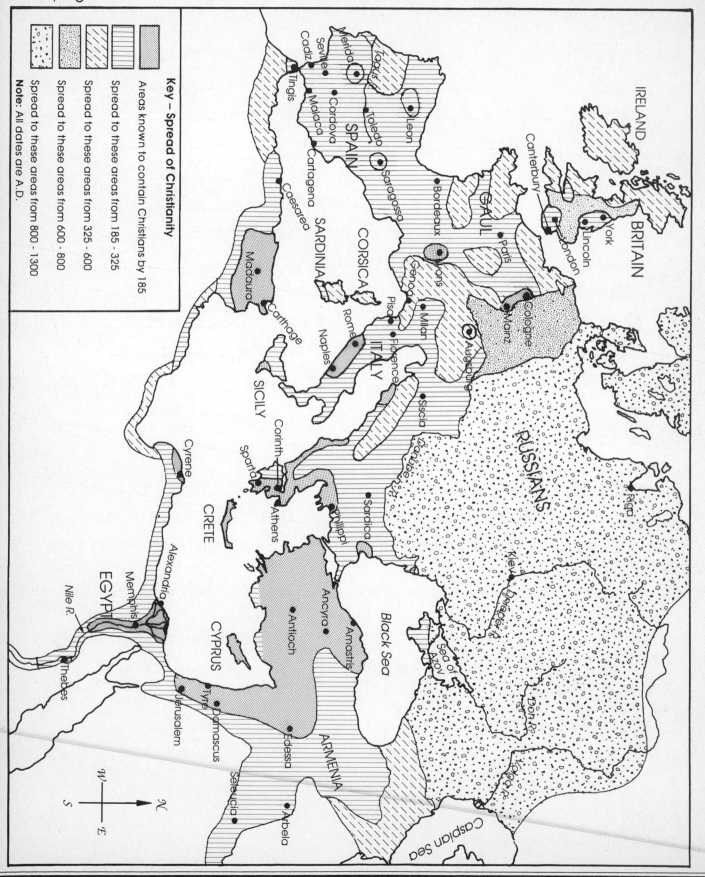

Key – Spread of Christianity

Areas known to contain Christians by 185

Spread to these areas from 185 - 325

Spread to these areas from 325 - 600

Spread to these areas from 600 - 800

Spread to these areas from 800 - 1300

Note: All dates are A.D.

IRELAND

BRITAIN

Canterbury
York
Lincoln
London

GAUL
Paris
Bordeaux
Lyons
Genoa

Cologne
Mainz
Augsburg

RUSSIANS

Kiev
Dnieper R.
Riga

SPAIN
Cadiz
Seville
Merida
Tagus
Corduva
Malaca
Cartagena
Caesarea
Toledo
Saragossa
Leon
Tingis

SARDINIA
CORSICA
Madaura
Carthage
Rome
Naples
Pisa
Florence
Milan
Siscia
ITALY

SICILY

Cyrene

CRETE

Corinth
Sparta
Athens
Philippi
Saratica

Danube R.

Black Sea

Sea of Azov
Don R.
Caspian Sea
Volga R.

Alexandria
Memphis
Nile R.
Thebes
EGYPT

CYPRUS
Antioch
Ancyra
Amastris

ARMENIA
Jerusalem
Tyre
Damascus
Edessa
Seleucia
Arbela

N
W   E
S

Spread of Christianity (Continued)

Name _____

Use the map on page 45 and a modern map to answer the questions.

1. Fill in the blanks with the correct years to show when Christianity spread to these areas.

   A. Thebes _____
   B. Naples _____
   C. Seleucia _____
   D. Madaura _____
   E. Siscia _____
   F. York _____
   G. Sparta _____
   H. Kiev _____
   I. Alexandria _____
   J. Genoa _____

   K. Paris _____
   L. Antioch _____
   M. Arbela _____
   N. Jerusalem _____
   O. Amastris _____
   P. London _____
   Q. Cyrene _____
   R. Bordeaux _____
   S. Riga _____
   T. Damascus _____

2. The city of Antioch is _____ of Ancyra.

3. The city of Kiev is located near the _____ River.

4. The Don River flows into the Sea of _____ .

5. Label these bodies of water on the map: Atlantic Ocean, North Sea, Baltic Sea, Mediterranean Sea, and Red Sea.

6. Use a red crayon to lightly color in the area where Christianity existed in 185.

7. Use a blue crayon to lightly color in the areas where Christianity spread between 185 and 325.

8. Use a yellow crayon to lightly color in the areas where Christianity spread between 325 and 600.

9. Use a green crayon to lightly color in the areas where Christianity spread between 600 and 800.

10. Use an orange crayon to lightly color in the areas where Christianity spread between 800 and 1300.

Expansion of Islam
to A.D. 750

Name _____

Use this map to answer the questions.

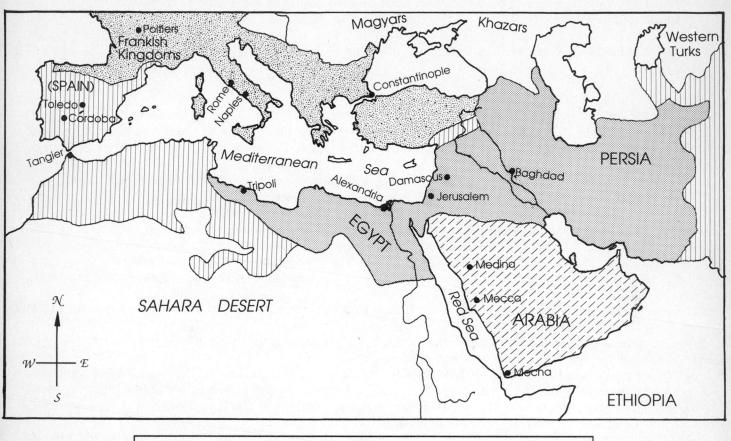

Key

▨ Conquests of Mohammed to 632	▥ Conquests of Omayyads to 750
▓ Conquests of Orthodox Caliphs (Muslim rulers) to 661	▦ Christian-held areas 750

1. Mohammed had conquered most of Arabia by the year _____ .

2. What Islamic group extended its influence into Persia? _____

3. By what year did the Omayyads extend the Islamic influence into Spain?_____

4. Place the correct letter in each blank to show if these cities were Christian-held areas
   (**C**) or Islamic-held areas (**I**).

   A. Mocha _____   F. Tripoli _____   K. Alexandria _____

   B. Damascus _____   G. Córdoba _____   L. Poitiers _____

   C. Rome _____   H. Naples _____   M. Mecca _____

   D. Baghdad _____   I. Medina _____   N. Tangier _____

   E. Constantinople _____   J. Toledo _____

China and India

Concept: Early civilizations developed in the Indus Valley of India and the Huang Ho Valley of China about 4,500 years ago.

Objective: The people in ancient China and India built cities at about the same time as cities were built in Mesopotamia and Egypt.

Vocabulary: civilization, Great Wall, Mongols, Mogul, Indus Valley, Huang Ho Valley, Khanate, Khan

Background Information:
- Buried brick walls discovered by scholars in the 1920's showed that cities existed in the Indus Valley between 2500 B.C. and 1700 B.C. These people had a highly developed way of life. They used bronze, silver, and copper to make pots, pans, and weapons. Gold was used for decorating objects. They carried on trade with people to the north and south.
- The Maurya Empire was India's first great empire. Chandragupta Maurya ruled the empire from 321 B.C. to 298 B.C. The empire covered nearly all of northern India, West Pakistan, and part of Afghanistan. His grandson, Asoka, extended the empire to include all of the Indian subcontinent, except a small part of the south.
- In about A.D. 320, the Gupta dynasty was begun in northern India. It lasted for almost 200 years. During this time, Indian civilization flourished. There were great advances in literature, art, sculpture, and medicine.
- The Moguls ruled India from 1526 until the early 1700's. The Portuguese were the first Europeans to arrive in India. Vasco da Gama reached India's southwest coast in 1498. English, French, and Dutch traders began to arrive in the 17th century.
- The Chinese had highly developed cities in the Huang Ho Valley during the 1700's B.C. They used writing similar to modern Chinese writing.
- Paper, porcelain, gunpowder, and the compass are a few of the many things the Chinese invented. Chinese ideas spread throughout the countries of east and southeast Asia.
- The many kingdoms of China were brought together in 221 B.C. by Shih Huang Ti. He standardized money, weights and measures, and the writing system. During his reign, he heavily taxed the Chinese people to obtain money to build roads and canals. His largest project was the Great Wall. The Han dynasty was founded in 202 B.C. by Liu Pang, after the fall of the Ch'in dynasty in 210 B.C.
- In 1211, an army of Mongols led by Genghis Khan invaded China. Eventually, this army conquered an empire that stretched across Asia into eastern Europe. In the late 1200's, the empire was divided into four parts. The largest part was ruled by Kublai Khan.

Teaching Suggestions

1. All of the activities for this chapter will be easier to do if the students have a modern physical map of Asia to use for reference. Point out the mountains, rivers, and desert. Begin with *The Han Empire, First Century B.C.*

2. The activity page *Empire of the Mongols* depicts Asia after Genghis Khan's empire had been divided.

3 *Empires in India* allows students to compare two maps of the same area during different periods of time.

Additional Activities

1. Find out how emperors of China and other countries were buried. Compare burial methods.

2. Have the students make a list of 5 to 10 Chinese inventions. Next decide their order of importance.

3. Have the students make charts comparing and contrasting the teachings of Confucius and Buddha.

The Han Empire,
First Century B.C.

Name _____

Use this map to answer the questions.

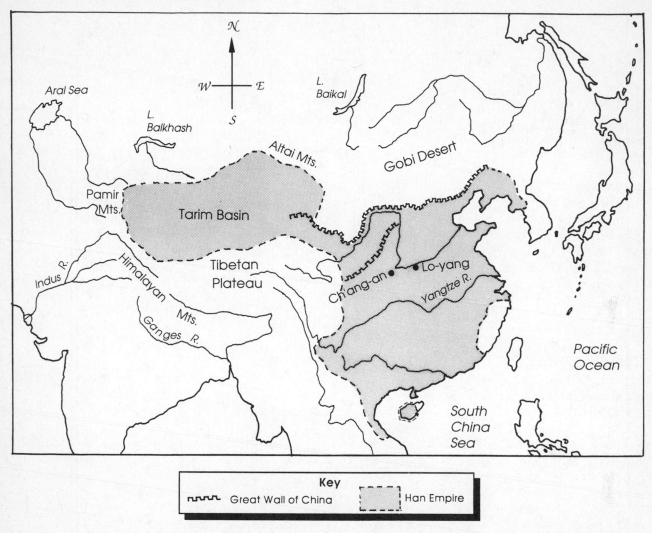

Key
rumru Great Wall of China   Han Empire

1. The broken line on the map shows the extent of the _____ Empire.

2. What man-made structure formed part of the empire's northern border?_____
_____

3. The _____ Desert was north of the Han empire.

4. Name the mountains found west and south of the Tibetan Plateau. _____

5. Name the two lakes shown on the map. _____

6. The Ganges River was _____ (which direction) of the Himalayas.

7. Which mountain range was north of the empire? _____

8. Was the Tarim Basin a part of the Han Empire?_____

9. Use a green crayon to outline the Han Empire.

10. Use a red crayon to trace the Great Wall.

Empire of the Mongols

Use with page 51.

Name _____

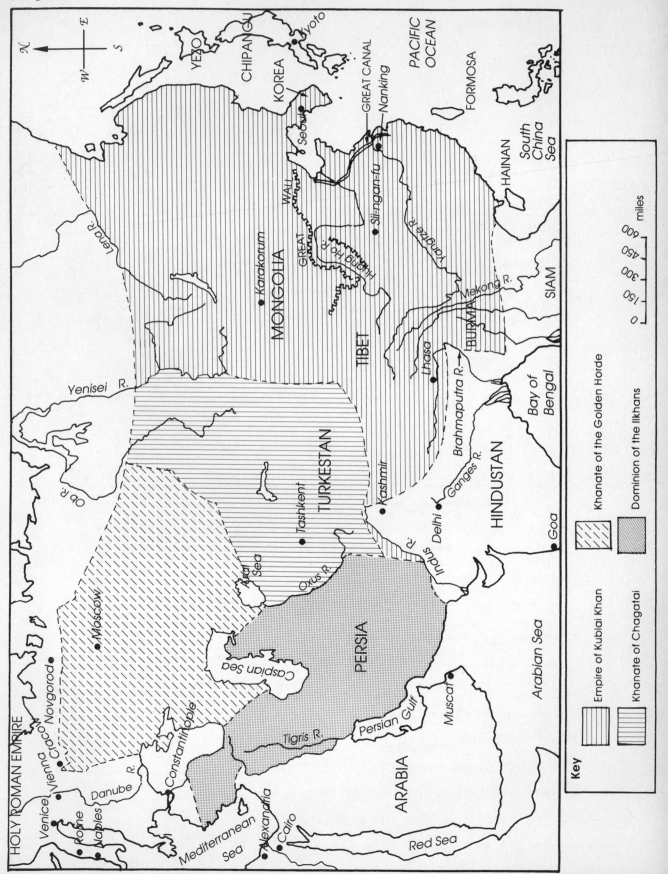

Key

- ▨ Khanate of the Golden Horde
- ▦ Dominion of the Ilkhans
- ▥ Empire of Kublai Khan
- ▤ Khanate of Chagatai

Empire of the Mongols (Continued)

Name _____

Use the map and scale on page 50 to answer the questions.

1. The Dominion of the Ilkhans was in a land called _____ .

2. Turkestan was under the rule of the Khanate of _____ .

3. What was built between the Great Wall and Nanking? _____

4. The _____ River emptied into the Bay of Bengal.

5. Turkestan and Persia were partially separated by the _____ River.

6. Name the area southwest of the Mekong River. _____

7. The _____ Sea was west of Hindustan.

8. Karakorum was in the part of Kublai Khan's empire called _____ .

9. Which of the empires on the map was largest? _____

10. Moscow was located in the Khanate of _____ .

11. The _____ Sea was west of Arabia.

12. Si-ngan-fu was part of the Empire of _____ .

13. Tashkent was part of the Khanate of _____ .

14. Use a ruler to measure the approximate distances between these cities.

    A. Nanking to Si-ngan-fu _____

    B. Karakorum to Nanking _____

    C. Delhi to Tashkent _____

    D. Muscat to Goa _____

    E. Goa to Kashmir _____

    F. Moscow to Karakorum _____

15. Use a red crayon to outline the Empire of Kublai Khan.

16. Use a blue crayon to trace the Great Wall and the Great Canal.

17. Use a green crayon to outline the Khanate of Chagatai.

18. Use a yellow crayon to outline the Khanate of the Golden Horde.

19. Use an orange crayon to outline the Dominion of the Ilkhans.

Empires in India

Name _____

Use these maps to answer the questions.

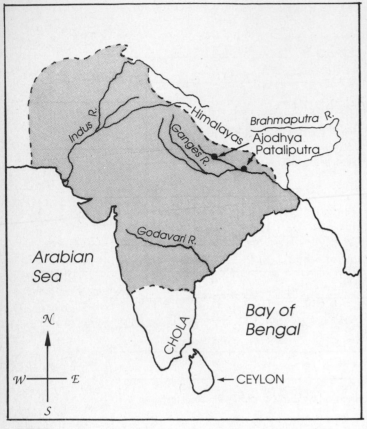

Maurya Empire 250 B.C.

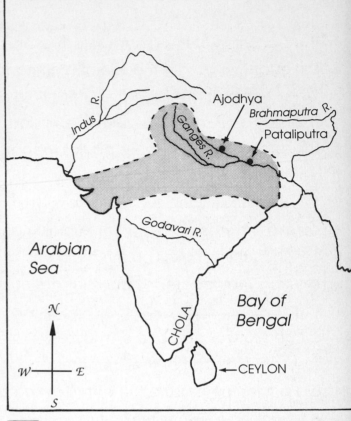

Gupta Empire A.D. 400

1. Was Chola part of the Maurya Empire? _____

2. The mountains northeast of the Maurya Empire were the _____

3. Pataliputra was near the _____ River.

4. Was Ceylon part of either empire? _____

5. Which empire was larger? _____

6. The _____ River was south of the Ganges River.

7. Name the river northeast of the Gupta Empire. _____

8. The _____ River was in the western part of the Maurya Empire.

9. Name the body of water west of Chola. _____

10. Name the body of water northeast of Ceylon. _____

11. Outline the Maurya Empire with a red crayon.

12. Outline the Gupta Empire with a green crayon.

The African Continent

Concept: Africa is a continent with many different ways of life.

Objective: Africa is a large continent with a variety of vegetation, climates, and ways of life.

Vocabulary: cassava, taro, yams, millet, sisal, myrrh, frankincense, Bedouin, nomad, rural, rain forest, savanna, caravan

Background Information:
- Africa is a continent which combines traditional and modern ways of life. In many parts of rural Africa, people still live much as their ancestors did hundreds of years ago. However, since the mid-1900's, many Africans have moved to the cities where living is more modern.
- Farming in Africa for the most part is still done with hoes and hand tools. Plows are most often drawn by horses, mules, camels, or cattle. Many farmers in Africa now grow surplus crops to sell. Since much of Africa is desert, the land must be irrigated.
- Deserts cover approximately two-fifths of Africa. It also has rain forests and savannas.
- The world's largest desert, the Sahara, covers an area of land in North Africa about as large as the U.S. Until the invention of airplanes and trucks, the only way to cross the Sahara was by camel caravan.
- Groups of people called Bedouins have lived in the desert of North Africa for thousands of years. They are nomads who move around in search of water and pasture for their herds of goats, camels, and sheep.
- Africa's straight coastline and its lack of navigable rivers hindered colonial penetration and, as a result, the interior of Africa was unknown for thousands of years. Europeans did not begin to explore the continent and establish colonies until the 1800's.
- Africa can be divided into eight cultural areas. These areas were determined by the surface features and climatic conditions which have affected the peoples' ways of life.

Teaching Suggestions

1. *Explorers in Africa* shows eight different expeditions. Having a physical map of Africa available will help the students see the variety of surface features and vegetation the explorers confronted. Tell the class that many of Africa's rivers are not easily navigable; many contain rapids and waterfalls. The rain forests, desert, and savannas made travel very difficult.

2. *Sub-Saharan Africa* shows many of the physical features of the continent south of the Sahara desert. The desert separates the coastlands of northern Africa from the rest of the continent. Point out the equator to the students. They will need a ruler for this activity.

3. The last activity page, *Cultural Areas of Africa*, involves a map and a chart which lists the names of the peoples who live in each cultural area. It also shows the economic activities for each area.

Additional Activities

1. Divide the class into eight groups. Assign each group a different African cultural area as found on page 56. Have each group add additional information to the chart about its cultural area: housing, cities, types of government, etc.

2. Have the class construct a mural which depicts different styles of African dress and/or musical instruments. *National Geographic* magazines, encyclopedias, and books about Africa are good sources.

3. Have students compare the camel of Africa to the bison of Native America. On a chart, they should include information about the animals and in what ways they were used and needed.

Explorers in Africa

Name _____

Use this map and the map key to answer the questions.

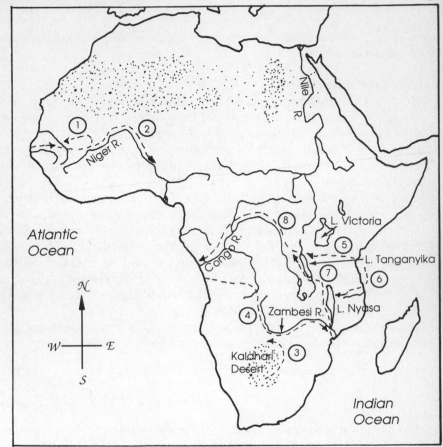

Key

① Mungo Park proved that the Niger River flows east–1795-1796.

② Mungo Park explored more of the Niger and drowned at Bussa Rapids–1806.

③ Livingstone's first trip, across the Kalahari Desert to Lake Ngami–1849.

④ Livingstone followed the Zambesi River downstream and named Victoria Falls–1855-1856.

⑤ Burton and Speke discovered Lake Tanganyika –1858.

⑥ Livingstone's third journey, with discovery of Lake Nyasa–1858-1863.

⑦ Livingstone to Lake Tanganyika–1866-1871. Found by Stanley–1871.

⑧ Stanley crossed to Atlantic, by way of Lake Tanganyika and the Congo River–1874-1877.

1. Which explorer showed that the Niger River flows east? _____

2. How, where, and when did Mungo Park die? _____

_____

3. In what years did Livingstone conduct an expedition which resulted in his naming of Victoria Falls? _____

4. Which two explorers discovered Lake Tanganyika? _____

5. Livingstone's first expedition took him across the _____ Desert.

6. Livingstone's third journey was during the years _____ .

7. Stanley crossed to the Atlantic by way of Lake _____

and the _____ River.

8. Who explored the farthest distance south on this map? _____

9. Who explored the farthest distance west on this map? _____

10. Use a blue crayon to follow the four expeditions taken by Livingstone.

11. Use a red crayon to follow Stanley's route to the Atlantic.

Sub-Saharan Africa

Name _____

Use this map and a ruler to answer the questions.

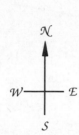

1. Name the two deserts in Africa.

   _____

   _____

2. The _____
   River is the southernmost river on
   the continent.

3. Meroe is on the banks of the

   _____ River.

4. _____ is an island in the Indian Ocean.

5. Name the five lakes on the map. _____

   _____

6. Name the two divisions of the Nile River. _____

7. The _____ is an imaginary line which passes through Africa.

8. Name the two cities between the Zambesi and Limpopo rivers. _____

   _____

9. Which direction is Malindi from Lake Victoria? _____

10. Use a ruler to measure the approximate distance between these cities.

    A. Malindi to Mogadishu _____ D. Sofala to Mombasa _____

    B. Gao to Luanda _____ E. Luanda to Mogadishu _____

    C. Timbuktu to Meroe _____ F. Meroe to Gao _____

Cultural Areas of Africa

Name _____

Use with page 57.

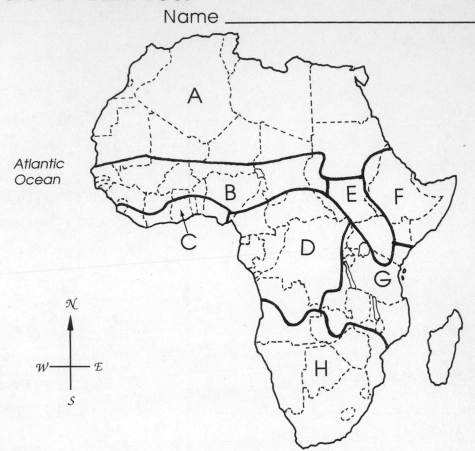

Atlantic
Ocean

Map Key

A = Northern Africa
B = Sudan
C = Guinea Coast
D = Congo Basin
E = Upper Nile
F = Eastern Horn
G = Eastern Africa
H = Southern Africa

Cultural Area	People	Economic Activities	
Northern Africa	Berbers Arabs	**Crops –**	grains, citrus fruit, olives, vegetables, cereal, cotton, date palms
		Other –	reserves of oil, natural gas, and water
Sudan	Susu, Mandingo, Beja, Nubian, Fulani, Wolofs	**Crops –**	vegetables, fruit, cereal
		Other –	metalworking, leather goods, trading, herds of cattle and camels
Guinea Coast	Ashanti, Fon, Ewe, Ibo, Yoruba	**Crops –**	taro, cassava, rice, maize, yams, bananas
		Other –	metalworking, raising pigs, chickens
Congo Basin	Bantu-speakers, Bambuti (Pygmies), Mongo, Bakongo, Baluba, Bena, Lulua, Tetela	**Crops –**	cassava
		Other –	metalworking, woodworking, copper and gold mining, hunting
Upper Nile	Nilotes (Nuer, Dinka), Shilluk	**Crops –**	millet, maize, sesame, beans, pumpkins
		Other –	herds of cattle, sheep, goats
Eastern Horn	Galla, Amhara, Konso, Sidamo, Afar, Somali	**Crops –**	cotton, barley, sorghum, millet
		Other –	herds of cattle, sheep, goats, salt mining, myrrh, frankincense
Eastern Africa	Watusi, Masai, Kikuyu, Chagga, Swahili	**Crops –**	cereals, fruit, tea, sisal, coffee, bananas, beans, corn
		Other –	herds of cattle
Southern Africa	Bushmen, Hottentots, Bantu, Zulu, Swazi, Sotho, Shona, Thonga	**Crops –**	grains, vegetables, fruit
		Other –	herds of horses, cattle, and sheep, diamond and gold mining

Cultural Areas of Africa (Continued)

Name _____

Use the map and chart on page 56 to answer the questions.

1. Which cultural area is between the Congo Basin and the Eastern Horn areas?

   _____

2. The Guinea Coast is _____ of the Sudan.

3. Eastern Africa is _____ of Southern Africa.

4. The Congo Basin is _____ of Southern Africa.

5. The northern one-third of the continent is covered by an area known as _____

   _____ .

6. Name the areas where cotton is grown. _____

7. Which area produces salt, myrrh, and frankincense?_____

8. _____ and _____ are mined in the Congo Basin.

9. The Fon and the Ewe live in a cultural area called _____ .

10. Which areas grow beans?_____

11. What economic activity do the Guinea Coast, the Sudan, and the Congo Basin have in
    common? _____

12. Which five cultural areas raise herds of cattle? _____
    _____

13. In the blanks, write the cultural area in which each of these peoples live.

    _____ A. Swazi   _____ I. Swahili

    _____ B. Galla   _____ J. Arabs

    _____ C. Bambuti   _____ K. Mongo

    _____ D. Berbers   _____ L. Bushmen

    _____ E. Shilluk   _____ M. Somali

    _____ F. Watusi   _____ N. Wolofs

    _____ G. Ashanti   _____ O. Yoruba

    _____ H. Susu   _____ P. Dinka

14. In the blanks, write the cultural area in which each of the economic activities takes
    place.

    _____ A. oil reserves   _____ E. leather goods

    _____ B. diamond mining   _____ F. sorghum

    _____ C. woodworking   _____ G. sisal

    _____ D. raising pigs   _____ H. pumpkins

Trade Routes

Concept: Trade between different areas involves the exchanging of products as well as ideas.

Objective: Trading products among different countries allows people to have items they cannot obtain locally.

Vocabulary: trade, caravan, Orient, export, import, commodity

Background Information:
- Contact between people in different parts of the world helped spread ideas and religion. Trade between regions allowed people to obtain and use items not available locally.
- Around 3000 B.C., Egypt exported gold, papyrus sheets, minerals, and grain to lands bordering the Aegean, Mediterranean, and Red seas. They were importing cedar, silver, iron, and horses from Syria, Lebanon, and other areas of southwestern Asia. By about 2000 B.C., there was trade with the Hittites, Cretans, and the eastern Mediterranean area. Through the Red Sea, there was trade with India, Punt, and Arabia for ivory, gold, spices, and grain.
- Alexander the Great's victories and the establishment of Greek dependent states provided the base for a worldwide trading area. Alexandria and Seleucia became international trade centers. Trade was carried on with India, China, Arabia, and the interior of Africa.
- Peace during the reign of Augustus (27 B.C.-A.D.14) was the basis for Roman trade. Rome became the center of a vast network of roads. Canals helped extend rivers into the interior of Italy. Harbor and docking facilities were built. Long-distance trade included Britannia, Germania, and southeastern Europe. Trade connected all parts of Africa. Caravans brought trade to the Orient. At this time, trade was conducted by full-time traders who were assisted by offices, bookkeepers, and agents.
- Explorers and traders came from Europe and the Arabian Peninsula to the coast of Africa. Cities grew up on sites where there were harbors. The traders took ivory, copper, and iron to the Middle East and the Orient. From the Orient, they brought back silks, glassware, and spices. Across northwestern Africa, trade was carried on between cities. The goods were transported on the backs of camels traveling in caravans.

Teaching Suggestions

1. If possible, obtain pictures of any products listed on the activity page map keys in this unit which you do not believe all students will recognize, such as myrrh, frankincense, or papyrus. Make an introductory bulletin board with these pictures.

2. Each of the four activity pages in this chapter shows the variety of products exported and imported by each area. Be sure students understand the difference between exports and imports. For the activity page *African Trade Routes* students will need a ruler.

3. Remind students that the U.S. was not the only country that traded for slaves. Traders in the Hellenistic and Roman periods obtained slaves through trade from places other than Africa, such as Germania and Hispania.

Additional Activities

1. Have students discover what items are exported from their state. They could make a chart which shows pictures of the products.

2. Have students choose five imported items they use or wear and find out where they were made. Then have them find five items they have that were made in their own country.

3. Divide students into groups. Have each group choose one item and figure out how many countries are involved with the production and functioning of the item (e.g., clock – made in Switzerland, batteries made in U.S., plastic cover on clock made in Taiwan, alarm made in Korea, etc.)

Egyptian Trade Routes

Name _____

Use this map to answer the questions.

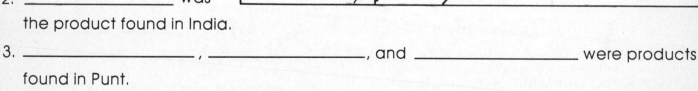

Map Key

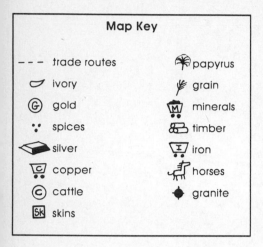

- - - trade routes
- ✎ ivory
- Ⓖ gold
- ∴ spices
- ◣ silver
- 🛒 copper
- ⓒ cattle
- Sk skins
- 🌴 papyrus
- 🌾 grain
- M minerals
- 📚 timber
- ⚒ iron
- 🐎 horses
- ● granite

1. Name the four products found in Lebanon.

   _____

   _____

   _____

   _____

2. _____ was the product found in India.

3. _____, _____, and _____ were products found in Punt.

4. Which four products were found in Egypt? _____

   _____

5. Name the country south of Egypt where ivory, skins, copper, cattle, and spices were exported. _____

6. Through which two cities did the route from Babylonia to Tashkent pass? _____

   _____

7. In Egypt, the trade routes were along the _____ River.

8. The trade route in India ended at the city of _____.

9. _____ were products found south of the Asian city, Merv.

10. Which product was found at the southern tip of the Blue Nile? _____

11. _____ was mined near Napata.

The Economy of the Hellenistic Period

Name _____

Use this map and the map key to answer the questions.

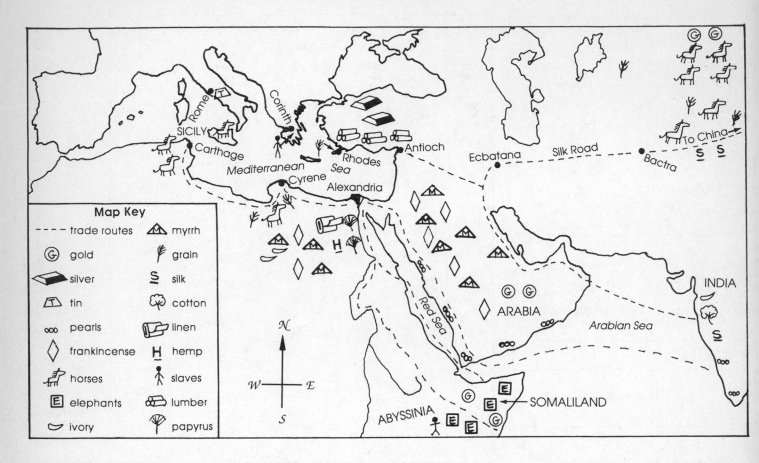

1. The direct trade routes between Arabia and India crossed the _____ .

2. The product found on Sicily was _____ .

3. Name the product north of Antioch. _____

4. Name the road between Ecbatana and Bactra. _____

5. _____ was mined near Rome.

6. What product was grown near Rhodes?_____

7. Name the two products found south of Cyrene. _____

8. What three things were traded in Abyssinia and Somaliland? _____

_____

9. Besides pearls, what items were found in India?_____

10. Papyrus was found south of the city of _____ .

11. In how many locations was myrrh found? _____

12. What three products were found north of the road to China?_____

_____

Economic Life in the Roman Empire

Name ____________________________

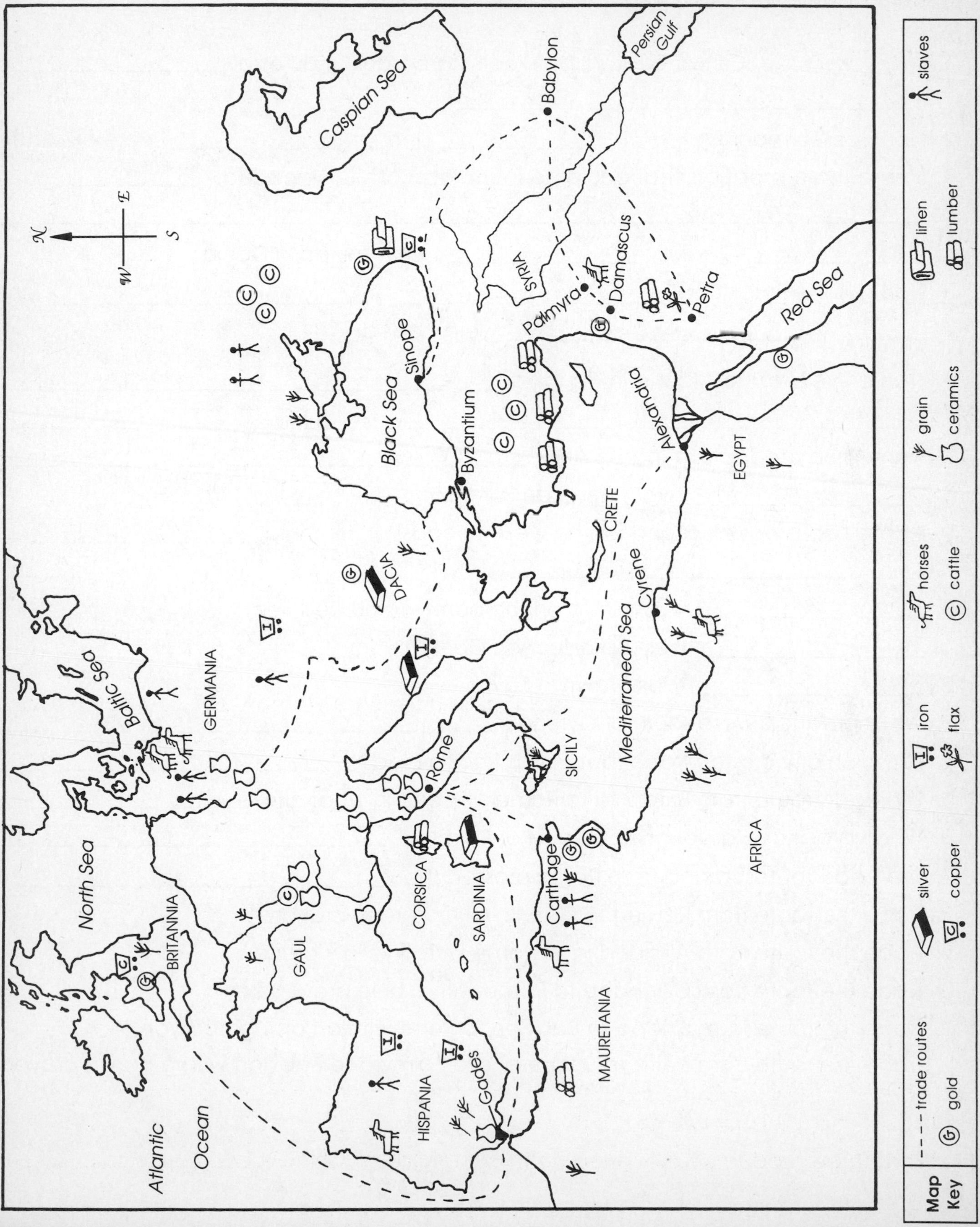

Caspian Sea
Persian Gulf
Babylon
SYRIA
Damascus
Palmyra
Petra
Red Sea
Black Sea
Sinope
Byzantium
Alexandria
EGYPT
CRETE
Cyrene
Mediterranean Sea
DACIA
Baltic Sea
GERMANIA
Rome
SICILY
Carthage
AFRICA
CORSICA
SARDINIA
North Sea
BRITANNIA
GAUL
MAURETANIA
HISPANIA
Gades
Atlantic Ocean
N
E
S
W
Map Key
trade routes
gold
silver
copper
iron
flax
horses
cattle
grain
ceramics
linen
lumber
slaves

Use with page 62.

Economic Life in the Roman Empire

(Continued)   Name _____

Use the map and map key on page 61 to answer the questions.

1. What two products were found between Damascus and Petra? _____
   _____

2. North of Germania, _____ and _____ were exported.

3. Name three products that could be found east of the Black Sea. _____
   _____

4. _____ and _____ were mined in Dacia.

5. North of the Black Sea, _____ , _____ , and
   _____ were traded.

6. Name five products found in Hispania. _____
   _____

7. Name two products found on Sicily. _____

8. _____ was mined on Sardinia.

9. Name two products found on the western coast of Britannia. _____
   _____

10. _____ was mined on the banks of the Red Sea.

11. _____ was a product on Corsica.

12. _____ was grown in Egypt.

13. What products were south of Cyrene? _____

14. To which city did the trade route from Sinope lead? _____

15. The trade route from Britannia to Rome stopped in what city?_____

16. What product was found southeast of Palmyra? _____

17. The trade routes to and from Rome crossed the _____ Sea.

18. Trace the route from Rome to Britannia with a green crayon.

19. Trace the route from Alexandria to Rome with a yellow crayon.

20. Trace the route from Carthage to Rome with a blue crayon.

21. Trace the route from Sinope to Babylon to Petra with an orange crayon.

22. Trace the route from Petra to Damascus to Palmyra to Babylon with a brown crayon.

African Trade Routes

Name _____

Use this map and the scale to answer the questions.

Map Key
- ·—··—· Land Routes
- - - - - European Sea Routes
- ⓖ Gold Mines
- ⓢ Salt Mines

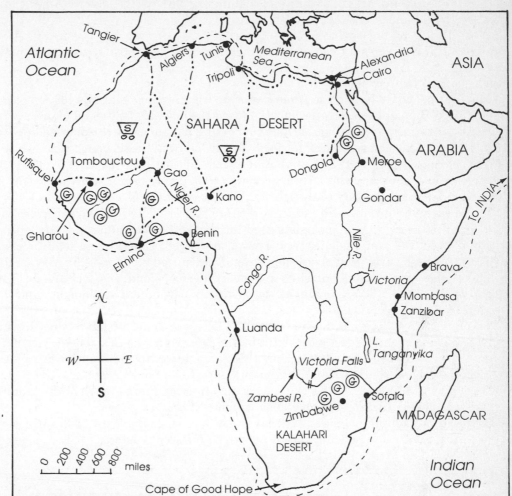

1. The dashes show _____ sea routes around Africa.

2. The sea route on the eastern side of Africa headed to _____ .

3. _____ was mined between Tripoli and Kano.

4. There were _____ mines west of Sofala.

5. What was mined northwest of Tombouctou? _____

6. Name the four Mediterranean coastal cities where European ships stopped.

_____

7. The _____ River is north of Luanda.

8. Victoria Falls is on the _____ River.

9. The _____ Desert is in southern Africa.

10. Use the scale to measure the approximate distances between these cities.

   A. Benin to Luanda   _____   E. Tangier to Tripoli _____

   B. Elmina to Kano   _____   F. Meroe to Mombasa _____

   C. Zimbabwe to Brava   _____   G. Alexandria to Zanzibar _____

   D. Cairo to Meroe   _____

Western Hemisphere

Concept: The earliest inhabitants of North and South America came from Asia.

Objective: Students are to understand that during the Ice Age, Native Americans followed animals from Asia to the New World and eventually settled there.

Vocabulary: Native Americans, Bering Strait, archaeological site, glacier, civilization, tribe, artifact

Background Information:
- The first people to live in the Americas came from Asia. During the Ice Age, ice sheets covered much of the Northern Hemisphere. The ice sheets caused the level of the oceans to drop. When the level of water in the Bering Strait dropped, a land bridge connecting Asia and North America appeared. Animals crossed the bridge into North America searching for food. People followed the animals.
- Archaeologists believe that Native Americans migrated here at least 12,000 years ago. Some scientists say these early people came anywhere from 20,000 to 40,000 years ago. Over thousands of years the groups moved south, some of them all the way to the tip of South America.
- These early inhabitants did not leave written records. They did, however, leave the remains of their lives at sites where they settled. Archaeologists used these clues to determine that early people made weapons and tools from stone, used fire, and made pottery. They also weaved, painted, and sculptured.
- Three of these early groups developed highly advanced cultures—the Mayas, the Aztecs, and the Incas.
- The Mayan civilization flourished in parts of Mexico, Honduras, El Salvador, Guatemala, and in all of present-day Belize. By 800 B.C., the Mayas were living in permanent settlements and the Mayan lowlands were completely settled.
- The Aztecs lived in Mexico. They founded the city of Tenochtitlan during the mid-1300's. It became the capital and was one of the largest cities built in pre-European America. The Aztecs built the last and greatest Indian empire during the early 1400's. They ruled a mighty empire in Mexico during the 1400's and 1500's and were the most warlike of the three civilizations in Central and South America.
- During the 1300's and 1400's the Inca civilization conquered much of the land in South America. Their civilization was one of the largest and richest empires in the Americas.
- By the time Columbus landed in what is now known as the West Indies, there were hundreds of tribes in North America. Each tribe had a different name and different customs.

Teaching Suggestions

1. Point out the Bering Strait on a globe or map. Explain to the class that during the Ice Age, a land bridge appeared which connected Asia and North America. Also point out the location of the Rocky and Andes Mountains. At first the early people migrated along these two ranges. The activity page *Early People in the Americas* can be used now.

2. The students will need a physical and political map of North and South America for reference for the activity page *Native Cultures of America*. This page shows the location of the three major civilizations developed by the early people in Central and South America, and also the location of certain tribes in North America.

Additional Activities

1. There is speculation that the Americas were discovered by people other than the Vikings or Columbus. Some evidence suggests that the Phoenicians and the Chinese were here earlier. Have the students research these ideas.

2. On a chart, have students compare the life of the Native Americans in North America before and after the Europeans came. You may wish to assign a different tribe to every two students.

3. Let students pretend they are Native Americans and have them keep journals. They should write about a typical day in their lives. Have them tell what kinds of Native Americans they are and include facts.

Early People in the Americas

Name _____

Use this map and a political map of the Americas to answer the questions.

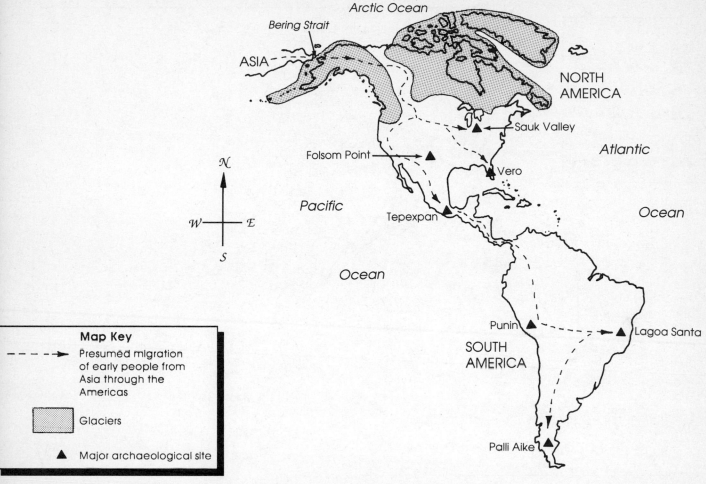

1. From which continent did the early people come?_____

2. To get from Asia to North America, the early people had to cross the _____ Strait.

3. Major archaeological sites on this map are marked with what symbol?_____

4. What covered much of what is now Canada? _____

5. Tepexpan was located in what is now the country of _____ .

6. Vero was located in what modern-day country? _____

7. Punin was located on the _____ coast of South America.

8. Was Palli Aike in southern or northern South America? _____

9. Name the continent where each archaeological site is shown.

   A. Palli Aike   _____   D. Lagoa Santa   _____

   B. Sauk Valley   _____   E. Folsom Point   _____

   C. Tepexpan   _____   F. Vero   _____

Native Cultures of America

Name _____

Use this map and a political map of North and South America to answer the questions.

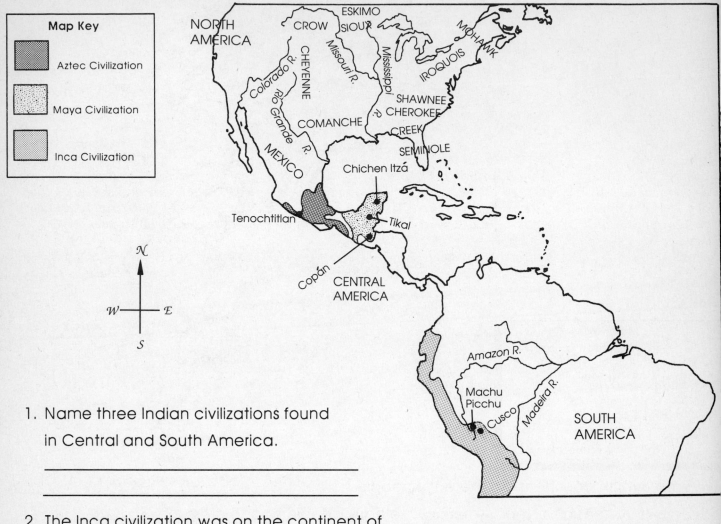

1. Name three Indian civilizations found in Central and South America.

   _____

   _____

2. The Inca civilization was on the continent of _____ .

3. The Maya civilization was found in _____ America and Mexico.

4. _____ was the site for the Aztec civilization.

5. The _____ lived in the northernmost part of North America.

6. The _____ tribe lived in what is now the state of Florida.

7. The Creek and Shawnee lived _____ of the Mississippi River.

8. The Crow lived near the _____ River.

9. Match the city to the civilization by placing the correct letter in the blank.

   Aztec = **A**   Maya = **M**   Inca = **I**

   A. Machu Picchu _____   D. Tenochtitlan _____

   B. Chichen Itzá _____   E. Copán _____

   C. Cusco _____   F. Tikal _____

The World Today

Concept: Today the land on five of the seven continents is subdivided into many countries.

Objective: Students will identify the many countries and other important places located on the continents as they are today.

Vocabulary: continent, country, state, territory

Background Information:

North America's area is 9,358,000 square miles. There are more than 427,000,000 people living on the continent. It is the third-largest continent and contains the countries and islands located north of the Isthmus of Panama.

South America's area is 6,888,000 square miles. It is the fourth-largest continent. The population of South America is 297,000,000. There are 12 countries on the continent and also the French overseas department of French Guiana.

Australia, the smallest continent, is 2,966,150 square miles. It is the only continent occupied by a single nation. Its population is 16,365,000. It is divided into six states, two mainland territories, and various external territories. New Zealand, a country southeast of Australia, is part of a large island group called Polynesia. It has two major islands: North Island and South Island. (New Zealand has been included with Australia on an activity page for the convenience of study.)

Africa, the second-largest continent, covers 11,683,000 square miles. Africa's population is 643,000,000, making up about 10% of the world's population. The continent is divided into more than 50 nations and includes Madagascar and other smaller offshore islands.

Europe's total area is 4,062,000 square miles. It is the sixth-largest continent, with a population of 697,000,000. Europe is densely populated, except for the north.

Asia, the world's largest continent, has an area of 17,006,000 square miles. Asia's population is 3,172,000,000. It contains nearly 60% of the world's population.

Antarctica, the fifth-largest continent, is 5,500,000 square miles. It consists of two major regions: West Antarctica and East Antarctica. These regions are joined by an ice cap that is up to 13,000 feet thick. It does not have a permanent population.

Teaching Suggestions

1. The students will need a political map for each activity page. The activity sheets may be used in any order. Be sure the students have access to very recent maps for all continents. The names of many countries in Africa and Asia have changed in the last few years. In Europe, Germany is no longer divided into two parts. The U.S.S.R. has been dissolved and this area is now in a state of transition. Czechoslovakia has broken into two countries: Czech Republic and Slovakia.

2. Please note: Antarctica has not been given an activity page. Not all of the islands of North America are shown on the activity sheet for the continent. The external territories of Australia are not included on Australia's activity sheet.

Additional Activities

1. Have the students put the capital city in the correct location for each country.

2. Assign a different country to each student. In an oral presentation, each student will give facts about the country (population, climate, language, major rivers and mountains, highest and lowest points, flag, etc.) as well as the history of the country.

3. Let the students choose one or two countries where they would like to live someday. In a pararaph and/or essay, they must explain their choices.

4. Have each student pick a country and write 20 clues about it. Then have students read their clues to the class to see if they can guess which countries the clues describe.

5. Give students clues each day about particular countries. Have them try to figure out which country the clues describe.

6. Have students make a big chart comparing different countries. Have them include population, resources, animals, life-styles, customs, etc., on their charts.

North America

Name _____

Use this map and a political map of North America to do the following:

1. On another sheet of paper, number from 1–17. Then identify these places in North America.
2. Next list the letters A–G. Write the correct name for each body of water after each letter.

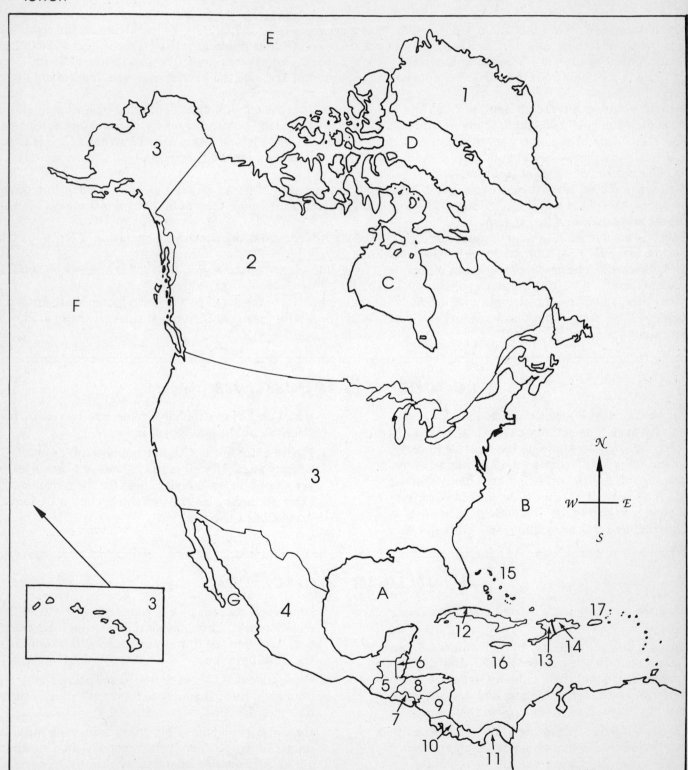

South America

Name _____

Use this map and a political map of South America to do the following:
1. On another sheet of paper, number from 1 – 14. Then identify these places in South America.
2. Next write the letters A and B and then name these bodies of water.

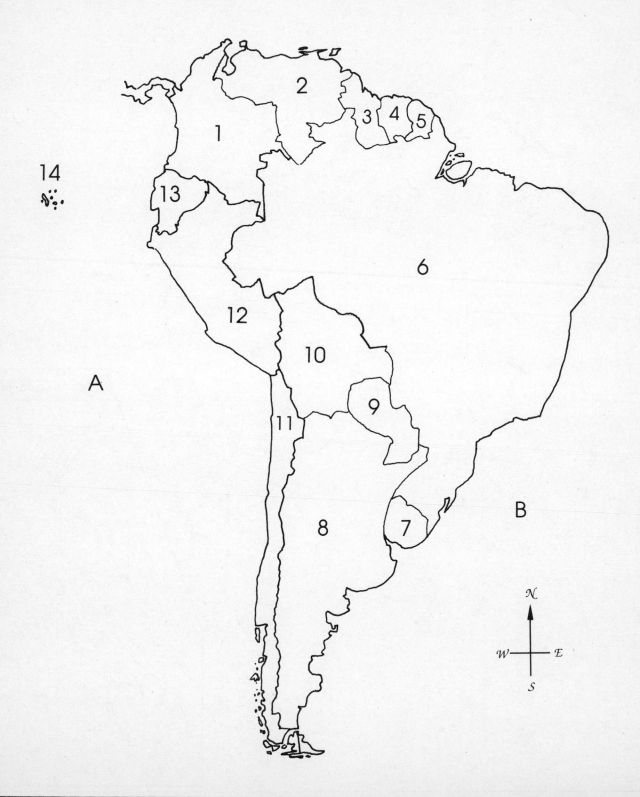

Australia (and New Zealand)

Name _____

Use this map and political maps of Australia and New Zealand to do the following:
1. On another sheet of paper, number from 1 – 10. Write the names of these places in Australia and New Zealand.
2. Next list the letters A – G. Write in the names of the bodies of water after each letter.

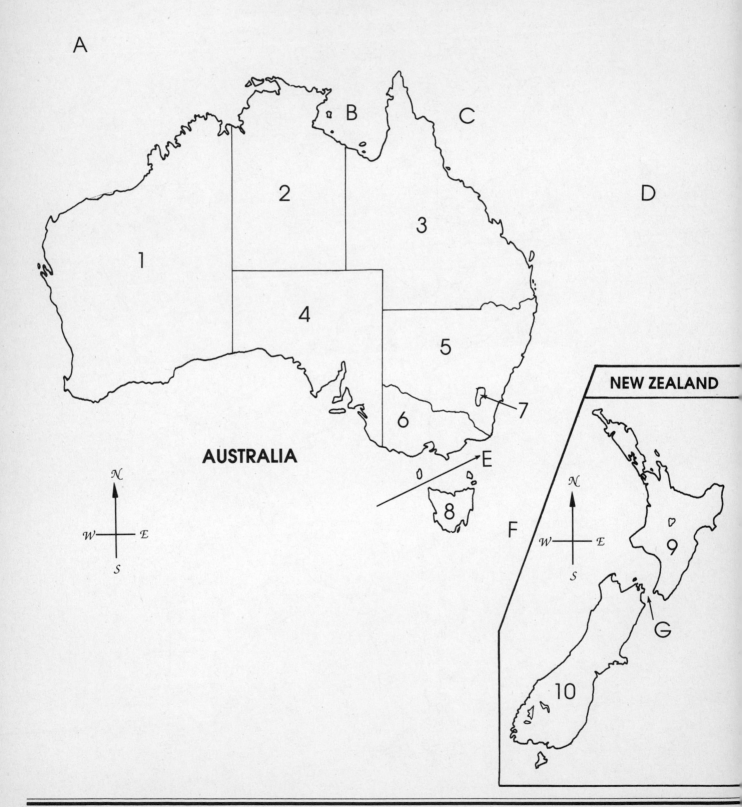

Africa

Name _____

Use this map and a political map of Africa to do the following:
1. On another sheet of paper, number from 1 – 56. Write the names of these places in Africa.
2. Next write the letters A – E. Write the name of each body of water after each letter.

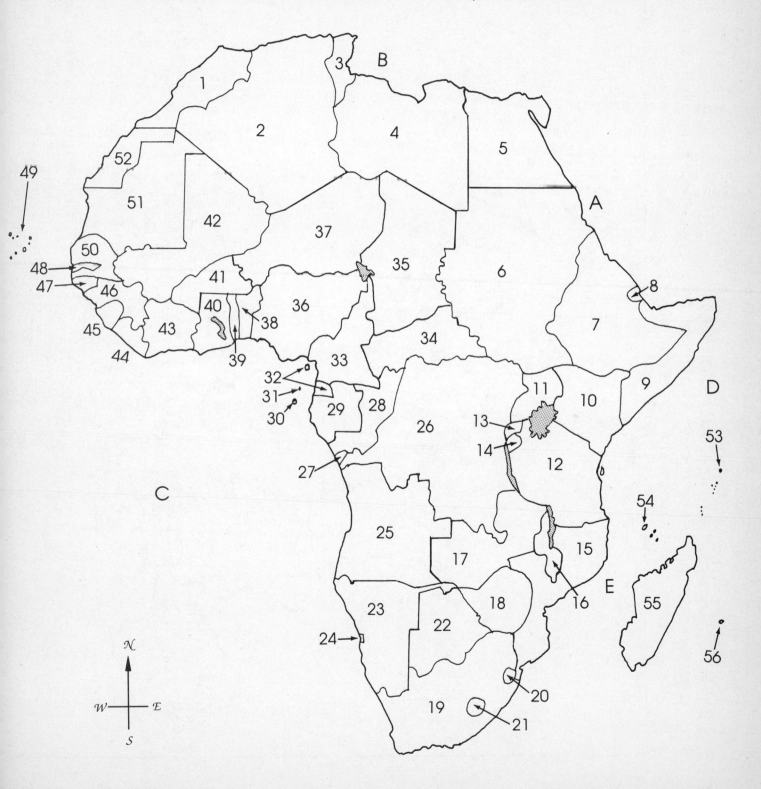

Europe

Name _____

Use this map and a political map of Europe to do the following:
1. On another sheet of paper, number from 1 – 37. Write the names of these places in Europe.
2. List the letters A – G. Write the name for each body of water.

Challenge: Draw in the borders within the former U.S.S.R. of those areas which have become independent countries.

Former

11 European

N
E
W
S

Asia

Name _____

Use this map and a political map of Asia to do the following:

1. On another sheet of paper, number from 1 – 42. Then write the names of these places in Asia.
2. List the letters A – H. Write the names of these bodies of water.

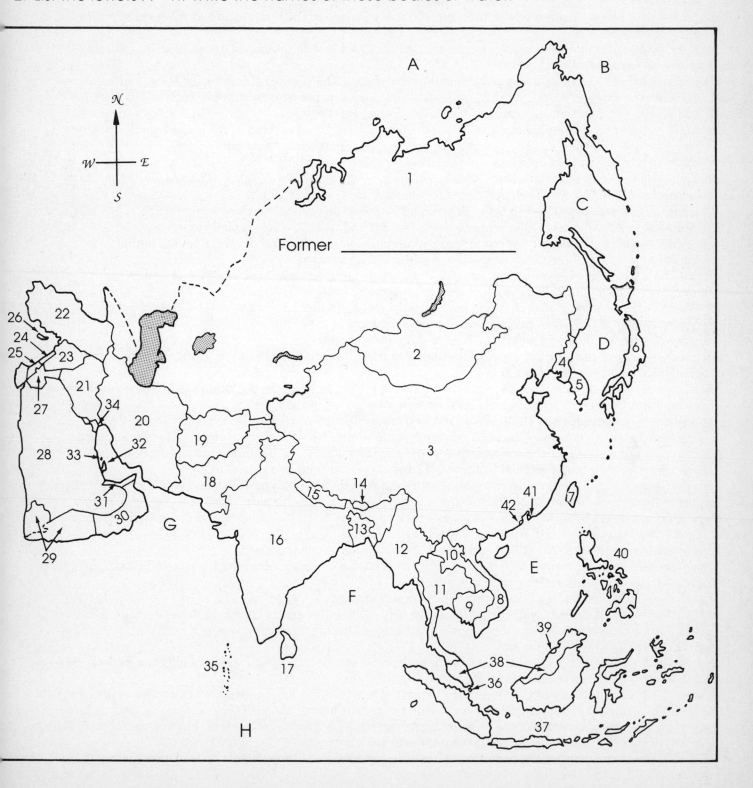

Former _____

Glossary

allied state — in ancient Greece, a state which was dominated by Athens and joined together with it in a league

animal husbandry — the care and raising of domesticated animals, such as cattle, horses, and sheep

aqueduct — an ancient structure of channels raised on one or more series of arches for carrying a city's water supply

archaeological site — a place where the scientific study is done of the past culture as revealed by relics left by ancient peoples

artifact — an object showing human workmanship; such as a tool or weapon of archaeological interest

artisan — a person skilled in a craft

Australopithecus — earliest group of humanlike creatures, with evidence of intelligence (e.g. toolmaking)

barbarian — a member of a people or group which lived outside the Roman Empire, such as the Goths, Vandals, and Huns; a civilization regarded as primitive, savage, etc.

Bedouin — an Arab belonging to one of the wandering desert tribes of Arabia, Syria, and northern Africa

Bering Strait — the shallow body of water between Alaska and the Soviet Union

caravan — a company of people traveling together for safety; especially across deserts

cassava — a tropical plant with large, thick roots from which an edible starch is obtained

Christianity — the Christian religion based on the teachings of Jesus Christ

Christians — persons professing belief in the religion based on the teachings of Jesus Christ

citizen — a person who owes allegiance to a government and is entitled to its civil rights

city-state — a state in ancient Greece made up of an independent city and the territory surrounding it

civilization — an advanced stage of social and cultural development

clan — an early form of social group, composed of several families claiming a common ancestor

commodity — in commerce, any product that is bought and sold

conquest — the acquiring of something, such as property, by force

continent — any of the seven principal landmasses on earth

country — a nation covering an area of land with specific boundaries

Crusades — any of the military expeditions undertaken by Christians in the 11th, 12th, and 13th centuries to recover the Holy Land from the Moslems

Dead Sea Scrolls — ancient manuscripts from Palestine found in a cave in the Qumran Valley near the western shore of the Dead Sea; more scrolls were found later in other caves in the area

democracy — government by the people, exercised either directly or through elected representatives

dependent state — in Ancient Greece, a group of people who relied on the controlling nation for support

empire — a number of territories or nations under the jurisdiction and dominion of one ruler

equal-area map — a map designed to show the accurate size of land and water areas

equator — an imaginary line encircling the earth's surface, dividing the northern and southern hemispheres

export — sending items out of one country to another, especially for the purpose of sale

Fertile Crescent — a historic region of Asia, extending in an arc from the eastern coast of the Mediterranean Sea across Syria and Iraq to the northern coast of the Persian Gulf

flake tool — tools used in the Stone Age that were made from stone fragments

frankincense — a gum resin which burns freely and is used as incense; obtained from trees in Asia and Africa

frigid — extremely cold; lacking heat or warmth

glacier — a large mass of ice originating from compacted snow

Great Wall — the defensive wall that stretches nearly 4,000 miles across China; built to keep out invaders

hemisphere — any of the halves of the earth: northern, southern, eastern, or western

hominid — natural family of man

Homo erectus — ancient man; associated with early handaxe industries and was probably the first to use fire

Homo sapiens — modern man

Huang Ho Valley — valley of the Huang Ho River that starts in the Tibetan Highlands and flows into the Yellow Sea

ice sheet — a thick layer of ice covering an extensive area for a long period of time

imperial province — a portion of the Roman Empire governed by a representative of the emperor for an indefinite term

import — bringing goods from a foreign country into one's own country in commerce

Indus Valley — valley along the Indus River in southwestern Asia where a highly developed ancient culture flourished from 2500 B.C. to 1700 B.C.

influence — the power of a person or group to affect others

Islam — the Moslem religion, of which Mohammed was the greatest prophet

Jews — people descended, or regarded as descended, from the ancient Hebrews; their religion is Judaism

Judaism — the Jewish religion

Khan — a title given to Genghis Khan and his successors who ruled over Turkish, Tatar, and Mongol tribes and dominated most of Asia during the Middle Ages.

khanate — the dominion or jurisdiction of a khan

kingdom — a political and territorial unit headed by a monarch

Latin — the language of ancient Rome

latitude — an imaginary set of lines which tells the location of points north and south of the equator

longitude — an imaginary set of lines which tells the location of points east and west of the prime meridian

map — a precisely drawn picture of all or part of the earth

map projection — any flat-surfaced drawing that shows a globe's meridians and parallels

Mercator projection — a method of making maps on which the meridians are equally spaced and distance between the parallels of latitude becomes greater as the poles are approached; best type of map for finding directions

Mesopotamia — an ancient country lying between the Tigris and Euphrates Rivers, where the world's earliest civilization developed

Middle East — a large region covering parts of northeastern Africa, southwestern Asia, and southeastern Europe

millet — a grass whose small grain is used for food in Asia and Africa

Mogul — Muslim empire of India

Mongols — natives of Mongolia

Moslems — true believers of Islam

myrrh — a fragrant gum resin exuded from any of several trees and shrubs of Arabia and eastern Africa; used in making incense and perfume

Native Americans — original inhabitants of North and South America; Indians

Near East — countries near the east end of the Mediterranean Sea, including those of southwestern Asia and part of northeastern Africa; many refer to it as the Middle East

nomad — a member of a tribe, nation, or race moving about constantly, having no permanent home

Orient — Asia, especially eastern Asia; the Far East

peninsula — a long projection of land surrounded by water on three sides

prime meridian — the meridian of 0° longitude which runs from north to south, used to locate points east and west

prophet — a religious teacher or leader regarded as, or claiming to be, divinely inspired

pyramid — a huge structure with a square base and four triangular sides meeting at a point; built by the ancient Egyptians and used as royal tombs and temples

rain forest — a dense evergreen forest in tropical areas with an annual rainfall of at least 100 inches a year

republic — a state or nation in which the supreme power rests in all the citizens entitled to vote; citizens vote for officers and representatives responsible to them

rural — living in the country; having to do with farming; agricultural

savanna — a flat, treeless grassland in tropical or subtropical areas

scale — a unit of measurement that stands for another unit of measurement

senatorial province — during the Roman Empire, an area governed by proconsuls having an annual term

sewer — an underground pipe or drain used to carry off rainwater and waste matter

sisal — a strong fiber used for making rope and cordage

state — a territorial or political unit organized under one government

Stone Age — the earliest known period in human culture characterized by the use of stone tools

taro — a tropical plant cultivated for its starchy, edible root

temperate — neither hot nor cold climate

territory — a part of a country or empire that does not have all the rights of a major division

time zone — the official time in any of the earth's 24 regions

tomb — a vault or chamber for the burial of the dead

torrid — so hot as to be parching or oppressive

trade — the act or business of exchanging commodities for other commodities or for money

tribe — a group of persons, families, or clans sharing a common ancestry, language, culture, and/or name

tribute — money paid regularly by one ruler or nation to another

via — a Latin word for a way or road

yams — large, edible, starchy roots grown in tropical climates

Answer Key

Page 3
1. Antarctica
2. northern
3. (*color North America red*)
4. (*color Australia blue*)

Page 4
Continents in Eastern Hemisphere
  Europe
  Asia
  Africa
  Australia
  Antarctica
Continents in Western Hemisphere
  North America
  South America
  Antarctica
Continents in Northern Hemisphere
  Asia
  Africa
  Europe
  North America
  South America
Continents in Southern Hemisphere
  South America
  Antarctica
  Australia
  Africa
Oceans in Eastern Hemisphere
  Arctic Ocean
  Pacific Ocean
  Indian Ocean
Oceans in Western Hemisphere
  Arctic Ocean
  Pacific Ocean
  Atlantic Ocean
Oceans in Northern Hemisphere
  Pacific Ocean
  Arctic Ocean
  Atlantic Ocean
Oceans in Southern Hemisphere
  Pacific Ocean
  Atlantic Ocean
  Indian Ocean

Page 6
1. Mercator
2. equal-area
3. Mercator map
4. 0°
5. 0°
6. north
7. Sydney
8. Cape Town
9. western
10. 0° 30°E
11. Africa, Europe, Antarctica
12. 75°S
13. 0° and 30°W
14. Rio de Janeiro Buenos Aires
15. 15°N and 30°N
16. western
17. 120°W
18. 0°, 20°S, 40°S
19. Would use equal-area map
20. equal-area map
21. equal-area map
22. equal-area map
23. *artwork required*

Page 7
1. warm
2. middle
3. middle and low
4. South America, Africa, and Australia
5. Arctic
6. North America, Africa, Asia
7. middle
8. Antarctica
9. hot
10. *artwork required*

Page 9
1. one
2. 12 noon
3. 180°
4. no
5. east
6. 4:00 AM
7. one hour
8. 6:00 AM
9. 1:00 AM
10. 9:00 PM
11. 11 hours
12. 12 hours

13.

Longitude	Time
0°	12:00 noon
90°W	6 AM
120°E	8 PM
15°E	1 PM
135°W	3 AM
30°W	10 AM
105°E	7 PM
45°W	3 PM
75°W	7 AM
150°W	2 AM

Longitude	Time
135°E	9 PM
165°W	1 AM
60°E	4 PM
180°	12:00 midnight
75°E	5 PM
150°E	10 PM
105°W	5 AM
15°W	11 AM
120°W	4 AM
30°E	2 PM

Page 10

Distance in Miles Between Cities				
Cities	Boston	Miami	St. Louis	Chicago
Dallas	1550	1100	600	850
New Orleans	1300	600-650	600	800
Los Angeles	2500	2250	1550	1650-1700
Seattle	2450	2650	1650	1700
New York	150	1050	850	700
Washington	400	850	700	600
Pierre	1450-1500	1700	650-700	700
Salt Lake City	2050	2050	1150	1200-1250
San Francisco	2650	2550	1700-1750	1800-1850

Page 12
1. Stone Age
2. Africa, Europe, Asia, Australia
3. Australia
4. sapiens
5. 7
6. Homo erectus, Homo sapiens
7. erectus
8. Australopithecus
9. Indian Ocean
10.—12. *artwork required*

Page 13
1. ◖
2. yes
3. handaxes
4. flake tools
5. no
6. handaxes and flake tools
7. handaxes and flake tools
8.—10. *artwork required*

Page 14
1. B.C.
2. Altamira, El Castillo, Lascaux, Soultre, Grimaldi, Aurignac
3. 9
4. 200,000 B.C.
5. 4,000,000 B.C.
6. 30,000 B.C.
7. 1,750,000 B.C.
8. Homo erectus
9. 9000 B.C.

Page 16
1. Persian Gulf
2. Tigris and Euphrates
3. Nile
4. Mediterranean, Caspian, Red
5. Tutankhamen's
6. northwest
7. Thebes
8. Nile
9. A. Mesopotamia   D. Egypt
  B. Mesopotamia   E. Mesopotami
  C. Egypt
10. A. 190 miles   D. 900-925 mile
   B. 570-575 miles   E. 400-425 mile
   C. 850-870 miles   F. 780 miles

All distances are approximate.

Page 17
1. Fertile Crescent
2. △
3. Tigris and Euphrates
4. Jordan
5. A. E
  B. E
  C. E
  D. A
  E. E
  F. A
  G. E
6. 1. Red Sea
  2. Persian Gulf
  3. Caspian Sea
  4. Black Sea
  5. Mediterranean Sea
7.—9. *artwork required*

Page 18
1. Nile
2. south
3. garnet, turquoise, copper
4. alabaster
5. Red
6. Gold
7. Sandstone
8. limestone
9. 7
10. 6
11. A. W
    B. W
    C. E
    D. E
    E. E
    F. E
    G. W
    H. W

Page 21
1. Great   Mediterranean
2. Reuben
3. Levi
4. Asher
5. western
6. Benjamin
7. River Jordan
8. Hazor
9. Manasseh and Dan
10. Reuben
11. Phoenicians
12. Tirzah
13. Jabbok River and Yarmuk River
14. Great
15. Dan
16. A. 70 miles
    B. 40 miles
    C. 40 miles
    D. 70 miles
    E. 30-35 miles
    F. 80 miles
    G. 35-40 miles
    H. 95-100 miles
    I. 50-55 miles
    J. 110 miles

All distances are approximate.
Give students some leeway.

Page 22
1. Scythia
2. yes
3. Pasargadae   Persepolis
4. Cambyses
5. Cyrus
6. Arabia
7. Ecbatana
8. Susa
9. Darius I

Page 22 (Continued)
10. A. Red Sea
    B. Persian Gulf
    C. Indian Ocean
    D. Aral Sea
    E. Caspian Sea
    F. Black Sea
    G. Mediterranean Sea

Page 23
1. Ister
2. ivory   salt
3. ivory   slaves
4. Crete
5. gold
6. Cyprus
7. grain, silver, lead
8. Iberia
9. 1. Black Sea
   2. Mediterranean Sea
   3. Adriatic Sea
   4. Aegean Sea
   5. Atlantic Ocean

Page 25
1. Aegean, Adriatic, Mediterranean, Ionion
2. Rhodes
3. Cydonia, Knosses, Itanos
4. southern
5. Asia Minor
6. Olympus
7. Rhodes
8. 140-150 miles
9. A 100 miles
   B. 110-115 miles
   C. 50 miles
   D. 275-290 miles
10. A. 12 days
    B. 2 days
    C. 4 days
    D. 4 days

All distances are approximate.

Page 26
1. A. Cyprus   E. Sicily
   B. Iberia   F. Italy
   C. Scythia   G. Italy
   D. Greece   H. Iberia
2. A. 600 B.C. 8   E. 630 B.C. 7
   B. 720 B.C. 5   F. 734 B.C. 4
   C. 1300 B.C. 1   G. 658 B.C. 6
   D. 1200 B.C. 2   H. 900 B.C. 3

Page 27
1. A. A   E. D   I. D
   B. A   F. A   J. D
   C. A   G. D
   D. D   H. A
2. A. 60-65 miles   E. 235-240 miles
   B. 90-100 miles   F. 85-90 miles
   C. 360 miles   G. 65 miles
   D. 175 miles
3. *artwork required*

All distances are approximate.

Page 29
1. yes
2. visited the oracle of Zeus-Ammon
3. to honor him (answers will vary)
4. Babylon
5. yes
6. Black
7. 330 B.C.
8. Egypt
9. Crete
10. Asia Minor
11. Persian
12. Persepolis
13. Issus
14. 331 B.C.
15. A. 6   E. 7
    B. 5   F. 4
    C. 3   G. 1
    D. 2

Page 30
1. 1   6   3
   4   2   5
2. A. Turkey   D. Former U.S.S.R.
   B. Iran   E. Syria
   C. Afghanistan F. Iraq
3. A. 50°E 60°E   D. 70°E
   B. 30°E   E. 50°E
   C. 40°E   F. 50°E
4. *artwork required*

Page 32
1. Alps
2. Sicilia
3. Appia
4. Papilia
5. Valeria
6. Aurelia
7. A. 115-120 miles   D. 250 miles
   B. 120 miles   E. 275 miles
   C. 100 miles
8. *artwork required*

All distances are approximate.

Page 33
1. A. S   F. S
   B. I   G. I
   C. I   H. S
   D. I   I. S
   E. S   J. I
2. north

Page 33 (Continued)
3. Corsica, Sardinia   5. east
4. Creta, Cyprus, Sicilia

Page 34
1. extent of Roman Empire
2. yes
3. Rhine
4. Baltic Sea
5. Tigris and Euphrates
6. Corsica, Sardinia, Sicily, Crete, Rhodes, Cyprus
7. Caspian
8. Gaul
9. yes
10. *artwork required*

Page 36
1. Asia
2. Carthage
3. Rhine
4. Visigoths, Ostrogoths
5. Baltic
6. Gaul, Spain
7. A.D. 170
8. A.D. 451
9. Visigoths
10. Visigoths
11. Carthage
12. A. 6   D. 2
    B. 3   E. 5
    C. 1   F. 4

Page 37
1. A. E   E. W
    B. W   F. W
    C. W   G. E
    D. E   H. W
2. no
3. Huns Slavs
4. Rhine
5. no
6. A. 375 miles   D. 215-225 miles
    B. 850 miles   E. 750 miles
    C. 750 miles   F. 790 miles

All distances are approximate.

Page 38
1. A. Vandal   F. Franks
    B. Franks   G. Suevi
    C. Ostrogothic   H. Ostrogothic
    D. Visigoths   I. Franks
    E. East Roman   J. Ostrogothic
       Empire
2. *artwork required*

Page 39
1. English Channel
2. east
3. Irish
4. Strathclyde, North Wales, West Wales
5. Angles
6. Saxons

Page 39 (Continued)
7. Kent
8. Ireland
9. A. Mercia   F. East Anglia
    B. Northumbria   G. Wessex
    C. Mercia   H. Northumbria
    D. Kent   I. Essex
    E. Mercia   J. Sussex

Page 40
1. Pyrenees
2. Saxons, Lombards, Spanish March, Corsica, Balearic Is.
3. Wilzi, Wends, Bohemians, Moravians, Pannonian March, Croats, Bretons
4. Frankish
5. Rhine
6. Seine
7. Lombards

Page 43
1. David Solomon
2. fleet of ships, a large smelter
3. David
4. Jerusalem
5. David
6. Egypt
7. Megiddo
8. Chittim
9. Mediterranean Sea
10. Phoenicia
11. Jordan
12. Euphrates
13. Orontes
14. desert
15. A. 45-50 miles   D. 140 miles
    B. 95-100 miles   E. 40 miles
    C. 160 miles
16.–19. *artwork required*

Page 44
1. Dead Sea
2. Sea of Galilee
3. Gerizim
4. Olives
5. Nain
6. Caesarea Philippi, Seleucia, Bethsaida
7. Sharon
8. Jordan, Jabbok
9. Great
10. Judaea
11. cave

Page 46
1. A. 185-325   H. 800-1300
    B. by 185   I. by 185
    C. 185-325   J. 325-600
    D. by 185   K. 185-325
    E. 185-325   L. by 185
    F. 185-325   M. 185-325
    G. by 185   N. by 185

Page 46 (Continued)
    O. by 185   R. 185-325
    P. 185-325   S. 800-1300
    Q. by 185   T. by 185
2. southwest
3. Dnieper
4. Azov
5.–10. *artwork required*

Page 47
1. 632
2. Orthodox Caliphs
3. 750
4. A. I   H. C
    B. I   I. I
    C. C   J. I
    D. I   K. I
    E. C   L. C
    F. I   M. I
    G. I   N. I

Page 49
1. Han
2. Great Wall
3. Gobi
4. Himalayan
5. Balkhash, Baikal
6. south
7. Altai
8. yes
9.–10. *artwork required*

Page 51
1. Persia   8. Mongolia
2. Chagatai   9. Empire of
3. Great Canal   Kublai Khan
4. Ganges   10. the Golden Horde
5. Oxus   11. Red
6. Siam   12. Kublai Khan
7. Arabian   13. Chagatai
14. A. 600 miles
    B. 1350 miles
    C. 975-1050 miles
    D. 1200 miles
    E. 1200 miles
    F. 2625-2850 miles

All distances are approximate.

15.–19. *artwork required*

Page 52
1. no
2. Himalayas
3. Ganges
4. no
5. Maurya
6. Godavari
7. Brahmaputra
8. Indus
9. Arabian Sea
10. Bay of Bengal
11.–12. *artwork required*

Page 54
1. Mungo Park
2. He drowned at Bussa Rapids in 1806.
3. 1855-1856
4. Burton and Speke
5. Kalahari
6. 1858-1863
7. Tanganyika, Congo
8. Livingstone
9. Mungo Park
10.–11. *artwork required*

Page 55
1. Sahara, Kalahari
2. Orange
3. Nile
4. Madagascar
5. Chad, Victoria, Tanganyika, Rudolf, Nyasa
6. White Nile River, Blue Nile River
7. equator
8. Great Zimbabwe, Sofala
9. east
10. A. 450-500 miles
    B. 1900 miles
    C. 2375 miles
    D. 1150-1200 miles
    E. 2250 miles
    F. 2125 miles

All distances are approximate

Page 57
1. Upper Nile
2. south
3. north
4. north
5. Northern Africa
6. Northern Africa, Eastern Horn
7. Eastern Horn
8. copper, gold
9. Guinea Coast
10. Upper Nile, Eastern Africa
11. metalworking
12. Sudan, Upper Nile, Eastern Horn, Eastern Africa, Southern Africa
13. A. Southern Africa
    B. Eastern Horn
    C. Congo Basin
    D. Northern Africa
    E. Upper Nile
    F. Eastern Africa
    G. Guinea Coast
    H. Sudan
    I. Eastern Africa
    J. Northern Africa
    K. Congo Basin
    L. Southern Africa
    M. Eastern Horn
    N. Sudan
    O. Guinea Coast
    P. Upper Nile

Page 57 (Continued)
14. A. Northern Africa
    B. Southern Africa
    C. Congo Basin
    D. Guinea Coast
    E. Sudan
    F. Eastern Horn
    G. Eastern Africa
    H. Upper Nile

Page 59
1. timber, silver, horses, iron
2. grain
3. ivory, gold, spices
4. papyrus, minerals, grain, granite
5. Kush
6. Anau, Merv
7. Nile
8. Harappa
9. Minerals
10. timber
11. Gold

Page 60
1. Arabian Sea
2. horses
3. lumber
4. Silk Road
5. Tin
6. grain
7. grain, horses
8. slaves, elephants, gold
9. cotton, ivory, silk
10. Alexandria
11. 9
12. gold, horses, grain

Page 62
1. lumber, flax
2. horses, slaves
3. gold, linen, copper
4. gold, silver
5. grain, slaves, cattle
6. horses, slaves, iron, grain, ceramics
7. horses, grain
8. Silver
9. copper, gold
10. Gold
11. Lumber
12. Grain
13. grain, horses
14. Babylon
15. Gades
16. horses
17. Mediterranean
18.—22. *artwork required*

Page 63
1. European
2. India
3. Salt
4. gold
5. salt
6. Algiers, Tunis, Tripoli, Alexandria
7. Congo
8. Zambesi
9. Kalahari

Page 63 (Continued)
10. A. 1200-1250 miles
    B. 1000 miles
    C. 1800 miles
    D. 950-1000 miles
    E. 1100 miles
    F. 1600 miles
    G. 2800 miles

All distances are approximate

Page 65
1. Asia
2. Bering
3. ▲
4. glaciers
5. Mexico
6. United States
7. western
8. southern
9. A. South America D. South America
   B. North America E. North America
   C. North America F. North America

Page 66
1. Aztec, Maya, Inca
2. South America
3. Central
4. Mexico
5. Eskimo
6. Seminole
7. east
8. Missouri
9. A. I   D. A
   B. M   E. M
   C. I   F. M

Page 68
1. Greenland
2. Canada
3. United States
4. Mexico
5. Guatemala
6. Belize
7. El Salvador
8. Honduras
9. Nicaragua
10. Costa Rica
11. Panama
12. Cuba
13. Haiti
14. Dominican Republic
15. Bahamas
16. Jamaica
17. Puerto Rico
A. Gulf of Mexico
B. Atlantic Ocean
C. Hudson Bay
D. Baffin Bay
E. Arctic Ocean
F. Pacific Ocean
G. Gulf of California

Page 69
1. Colombia
2. Venezuela
3. Guyana
4. Suriname
5. French Guiana
6. Brazil
7. Uruguay
8. Argentina
9. Paraguay
10. Bolivia
11. Chile
12. Peru
13. Ecuador
14. Galapagos Islands
A. Pacific Ocean
B. Atlantic Ocean

Page 70
1. Western Australia
2. Northern Territory
3. Queensland
4. South Australia
5. New South Wales
6. Victoria
7. Australian Capital Territory
8. Tasmania
9. North Island
10. South Island
A. Indian Ocean
B. Gulf of Carpentaria
C. Coral Sea
D. Pacific Ocean
E. Bass Strait
F. Tasman Sea
G. Cook Strait

Page 71
1. Morocco
2. Algeria
3. Tunisia
4. Libya
5. Egypt
6. Sudan
7. Ethiopia
8. Djibouti
9. Somalia
10. Kenya
11. Uganda
12. Tanzania
13. Rwanda
14. Burundi
15. Mozambique
16. Malawi
17. Zambia
18. Zimbabwe
19. South Africa
20. Swaziland
21. Lesotho
22. Botswana
23. Namibia
24. Walvis Bay
25. Angola
26. Zaire
27. Cabinda
28. Congo
29. Gabon
30. Principe
31. São Tomé
32. Equatorial Guinea
33. Cameroon
34. Central African Republic
35. Chad
36. Nigeria
37. Niger
38. Benin
39. Togo
40. Ghana
41. Upper Volta
42. Mali
43. Ivory Coast
44. Liberia
45. Sierra Leone
46. Guinea

Page 71 (Continued)
47. Guinea-Bissau
48. Gambia
49. Canary Islands
50. Senegal
51. Mauritania
52. Western Sahara
53. Seychelles
54. Comoros
55. Madagascar
56. Mauritius
A. Red Sea
B. Mediterranean Sea
C. Atlantic Ocean
D. Indian Ocean
E. Mozambique Channel

Page 72
1. Iceland
2. Norway
3. Sweden
4. Finland
5. Former U.S.S.R.
6. Poland
7a. Czech Republic
7b. Slovakia
8. Hungary
9. Romania
10. Bulgaria
11. Istanbul
12. Greece
13. Crete
14. Albania
15. Yugoslavia
16. Austria
17. Italy
18. San Marino
19. Vatican City
20. Sicily
21. Malta
22. Sardinia
23. Corsica
24. Monaco
25. Switzerland
26. Liechtenstein
27. Germany
28. Luxembourg
29. Belgium
30. Netherlands
31. France
32. Andorra
33. Spain
34. Portugal
35. Great Britain
36. Ireland
37. Denmark
A. Mediterranean Sea
B. Adriatic Sea
C. Baltic Sea
D. North Sea
E. Bay of Biscay
F. Atlantic Ocean
G. Black Sea

Page 73
1. Former U.S.S.R.
2. Mongolia
3. China
4. North Korea
5. South Korea
6. Japan
7. Taiwan
8. Vietnam
9. Kampuchea
10. Laos
11. Thailand
12. Burma
13. Bangladesh
14. Bhutan
15. Nepal
16. India
17. Sri Lanka
18. Pakistan
19. Afghanistan
20. Iran
21. Iraq
22. Turkey
23. Syria
24. Lebanon
25. Israel
26. Cyprus
27. Jordan
28. Saudi Arabia
29. North and South Yemen
30. Aman
31. United Arab Emirates
32. Qatar
33. Bahrain
34. Kuwait
35. Maldines
36. Singapore
37. Indonesia
38. Malaysia
39. Brunei
40. Philippines
41. Hong Kong
42. Macao
A. Arctic Ocean
B. Bering Sea
C. Sea of Okhotsk
D. Sea of Japan
E. South China Sea
F. Bay of Bengal
G. Arabian Sea
H. Indian Ocean